LORENDO

LORENDO

―――

KENNETH WAYNE RINGER

EDITED BY KATIE JACKSON

WHITE ROCKET BOOKS

LORENDO

A White Rocket Book
www.whiterocketbooks.com

ISBN-13: 978-0692550618
ISBN-10: 0692550615

First printing: October 2015

0 9 8 7 6 5 4 3 2 1

ACKNOWLEDGMENTS

First, I have to thank my wife, Joyce, for her patience and encouragement, after asking me for years, "When are you going to finish the book?"

My major supporter, mentor, and advisor in this experience of writing a book was David Housel, our retired Athletic Director of Auburn University. Thank you, Housel.

Very helpful in my research for the Lorendo book was Kathy Bergman of the Iron Range Historical Society located in Gilbert, Minnesota. Kathy provided information on the early days of Gilbert and the Lorendo family. Thank you, Kathy.

I also would like to express my appreciation for the information provided by the sports information departments of the University of Minnesota (Duluth), Northern Iowa University, Presbyterian College, University of Georgia, and the archives department of the Auburn University Library.

While doing my research and trying to connect the dots in Gene Lorendo's interesting life, I was greatly aided by the treasure chest of scrapbooks, and newspaper articles about his athletic career. These scrapbooks and media records were kept by Gene's sisters, Adele and Lorraine.

Mac Lorendo, Gene's son, allowed access to this valuable information. Mac was very supportive of my efforts to write a biography honoring his dad. I was able to draw on his memory of many of the Lorendo stories. Also I'd like to thank Cam and Leah Lorendo for their interest and encouragement.

LORENDO

One unexpected source of information about Gene Lorendo's life up on the Mesabi Range was writer Tom Phillipich of Chisholm, Minnesota. Tom wrote a feature story on Gene Lorendo for a local newspaper. We enjoyed exchanging information and Lorendo stories.

Special thanks goes to my graphic designer, Jon Thompson, for his excellent detail work in designing the covers of the Lorendo book.

I must thank Betty Corbin for her computer expertise that helped me to complete this book.

A big thank you to Katie Jackson in editing this book for publication, making suggestions, and adding to its readability. I am thankful Katie shared the passion I possessed for writing the Lorendo book. Thanks Katie for your excellent work and professionalism.

I appreciate the advice and help I received from Larry Williamson.

A very important piece of the Lorendo story was provided by Thom Gossom, Jr in his book, *Walk On: My Reluctant Journey to Integration at Auburn University*. Thank you, Thom.

Last, I have to thank my son, John Ringer, and his close friend Van Allen Plexico, authors and Auburn graduates, who provided technical support, assistance, and aid in helping me to have my book published by White Rocket Books.

TABLE OF CONTENTS

FOREWORD

DAVID HOUSEL

Terms like "unique" and "one-of-kind" are thrown around so casually they have almost become trite, a cliché.

Not so with Gene Lorendo. With "Big Gene" they apply. He was unique. He was one-of-a-kind, the kind of man, athlete, and coach who will not pass our way again.

When he graduated from the University of Georgia in 1950 at age twenty-nine, he had already:

•Played eight years of college football;

•Played one year of professional basketball in the National Basketball League, forerunner to the NBA;

•Served three years in the Coast Guard; and

•Fought at Iwo Jima and Okinawa and was present at the USS Missouri when General Douglas McArthur accepted the Japanese surrender ending World War II.

All this in the eleven years since graduating from high school in 1939 at eighteen.

How could one man, unique and exceptional though he was, accomplish all this in just eleven years?

Ken Ringer will answer that question and tell you much more in his detailed, finely researched, lovingly written book on this one-of-a-kind man, the likes of which will not pass our way again.

And that's just the beginning.

LORENDO

After graduating from Georgia, "Big Gene" became assistant football and head basketball coach at Presbyterian College in 1950-51. When he left to join Ralph "Shug" Jordan's staff at Auburn in 1951, he was later replaced by Bo Schembechler, who would go on to win fame and glory at Michigan as Lorendo went on to win fame and glory at Auburn.

Lorendo served as one of Jordan's chief assistants for twenty-five years, recruiting and coaching Heisman Trophy winner Pat Sullivan and providing Auburn with some of the most prolific offenses in the history of the SEC at that time. His big, blustery, larger-than-life persona and his loud, deep, overpowering voice left an indelible impression on all who played for him, coached with him, even those who heard him from afar when he was on the practice field. It was said that one had never been cussed out until he was cussed out by Lorendo. And when you had been cussed out—or heard him cuss someone else out—you never would forget it.

Yet, underneath he was just a big ole Teddy Bear, a Huggy Bear, who appreciated the lure of the arts as much as he appreciated the grit and grind of college football, a man who loved his ballet son as much as his son who became an All-Southeastern Conference lineman and captain of the 1972 "Amazins."

Big Gene Lorendo was, indeed, unique, one-of-a-kind, the likes of which we will not see again. Ken Ringer has preserved this indelible man, this indelible personality, for generations to come. He has done a great service to all who love Auburn football, the SEC, and, most especially, to days of old.

David Housel

INTRODUCTION

Folks have asked the question, "Why are you writing a book about Gene Lorendo?"

My answer: Because it is a story that should be told.

I had the opportunity to get to know Gene Lorendo while he was coaching at Auburn. In the latter years of his life we developed a friendship, and I had a number of opportunities to visit with him. I found him to be one of the most interesting people I have met in my lifetime. There are more stories and tales about Lorendo than any other coach in Auburn football history. I have attempted to collect and re-tell a number of those stories in this book.

And I am not alone in believing that Lorendo's story needs to be told.

When Randy Walls, quarterback of the 1972 "Amazins" and "Punt Bama Punt" team, was informed I was writing this book, he stated, "It is about time someone wrote a book about Lorendo."

When I asked Tom Sparrow, the long-time director of athletic facilities at Auburn University, about his friend Gene Lorendo, he said, "Lorendo was the meanest and toughest SOB I have ever met in my life."

But Tom went on to say that three men had made a positive impression on him during his thirty-plus year career with the athletic department at Auburn University. One was Ralph "Shug" Jordan, Auburn's long-time legendary head football coach who laid the foundation for Auburn's football program. The second was Coach Pat Dye. (When asked in his job interview for the head football coach's position at Auburn how long it would take for Auburn to beat Alabama, Dye's answer was: "Sixty minutes." Coach Dye brought toughness, pride, and winning back to Auburn football.) The third person Tom Sparrow included among these giants of Auburn football history was Coach Gene Lorendo.

How did a man who grew up on the Mesabi Range of northern Minnesota end up coaching football for twenty-five years at Auburn University under the legendary Coach Shug Jordan?

Gene grew up loving sports and became an outstanding athlete in high school at Gilbert, Minnesota, where he excelled in football, basketball, and track. After attending four different colleges, playing professional basketball in the National Basketball League, and joining the Coast Guard in the middle of World War II (with stops at Pearl Harbor, Iwo Jima, Okinawa, and finally the surrender of Japan), he returned to Gilbert in February of 1946 where he met and married Jane Campbell, an English teacher and University of Minnesota graduate.

My biography of Gene Lorendo tells how he found his way to the University of Georgia where he played for Coach Wally Butts and his powerful teams of the forties. It tells how he missed out on an opportunity to play in the 1942 Rose Bowl, but did play in three bowl games—the Sugar (1946), Gator (1947), and the Orange (1948).

It goes on to tell how he led the SEC in pass receiving at Georgia in the 1949 season, where he also played basketball and ran track. He graduated from Georgia in 1950 with a bachelor's degree in education at the age of twenty-nine and was drafted by the Green Bay Packers.

This book recounts how, in 1950, Lorendo joined the staff of Presbyterian College as assistant football coach and head basketball coach, leading the Blue Hose team to one of its most successful seasons ever in basketball. And it tells the story of how, in the spring of 1951, Lorendo received a call from Shug Jordan inviting him to join the athletics staff at Auburn to coach the receivers (ends) and to be the resident manager of Graves Center, a complex of cottages that housed Auburn's scholarship athletes, where he was to keep those athletes under control and out of trouble.

That phone call was a turning point for Lorendo and marked the beginning of Gene's long and storied career at Auburn, where he coached a number of great receivers at Auburn including Jim Pyburn, Dave Edwards, Jerry Elliott, Jimmy "Red" Phillips, Jerry Wilson, Leo Sexton, Joe Leichtnam, Freddie Hyatt, Tim Christian, Howard Simpson, Terry Beasley, and Dick Schmalz. He also coached Thom Gossom, the first black player in Auburn history to letter and graduate from Auburn.

Gene was a member of the coaching staff in 1957 when Auburn won the national championship, and he recruited Pat Sullivan, who had a stellar career as a quarterback at Auburn and won the Heisman Trophy in 1971.

Maybe Lorendo's proudest moment at Auburn was in 1972 as offensive coordinator of the team called the "Amazins." This team, which many predicted would not win a single SEC game and for which Gene's son, Mac, was an All-SEC tackle and team captain, amazed everyone by winning ten games and losing only one. They defeated three top-ten rated teams and five teams rated in the top twenty-five in the country, the big one being Alabama, coached by Paul "Bear" Bryant and ranked at the time the No. 2 team in the country. Auburn kicked a field goal and blocked two punts in the last six minutes of the game to win 17-16.

Gene retired from coaching with Jordan in 1975. After living for thirty-two years in Auburn, he and Jane returned to their native state of Minnesota in 1983 to live in the resort community of Northome.

Gene passed away on Easter morning, April 15, 2001, in Atlanta where he had moved after Jane's death in 1996. But his story lives on in the memories of their three children—sons Cam and MacLean (Mac) and daughter Leah—as well as the many people whose lives he touched. His is a story worth telling.

Some of the People Appearing in this Book

Jack Dempsey

Tom Laundry

"Bo" Schembechler

Hank Luisetti

Frank Broyles

General Douglas McArthur

Wally Butts

Andy Griffith

Gen. "Howling Mad" Smith

Charlie Trippi

Roy Skinner

Adolph Rupp

Bobby Dodd

Norm Sloan

Dick McPhee

Lewis Grizzard

Paul "Bear" Bryant

Charlie "Choo Choo" Justice

Ralph McGill

Joe Lewis

Don Knotts

Marion Gilbert

Ralph "Shug" Jordan

Pat Sullivan

Tucker Frederickson

Terry Beasley

Bill Newton

Lloyd Nix

Charlie Waller

Tommy Lorino

Jimmy "Red" Phillips

Pat Dye

Mac Lorendo

Randy Walls

Terry Henley

James Owens

Thom Gossom

Ken Rice

Bill Van Dyke

Richard Guthrie

C.L. "Shot" Senn

Dick Schmalz

Connie Frederick

Lee Cannon

Jerry Smith

Jim Dozier

Paul Davis

Buck Bradberry

Leah Rawls Atkins

Tim Christian

Sam Mitchell

Chris Davis

Erk Russell

Mike Currier

Joe Connally

David Housel

Monk Gafford

Ed Dyas

CHAPTER ONE:

COACH LORENDO
AND CONNIE FREDERICK:
THE MAKING OF
IRON BOWL LEGENDS

Auburn vs Alabama, Legion Field, Birmingham
November 30, 1969

A win over Paul "Bear" Bryant, whose Alabama Crimson Tide team had won the Iron Bowl five years in a row, would give Auburn an 8-2 record. Connie Frederick, a senior wide receiver and punter, was a serious student of the game. He spent hours watching Auburn's opponents in the film room.

As Frederick studied Alabama's punt return scheme, he noticed the right end charged in two or three steps, then peeled off and ran downfield to set up the blocking for their All-American back, Johnny Musso. Frederick asked Coach Gene Lorendo, the Tigers' offensive coordinator, to sit down and view the Alabama films with him. He focused on the punt coverage and convinced Lorendo this could be a big play opportunity for Auburn.

Gene raised the idea of a fake punt in the coaches' staff meeting. He emphasized Frederick's speed and running ability as a factor.

Excited by the possibility, Frederick told several teammates about it and hounded Coach Lorendo all week: "Coach, we've got to run the fake punt Saturday." Lorendo later reported that he and Frederick developed a signal for the play. When Frederick went

back to punt, he was to glance over to Coach. If the fake was on, Gene would nod.

Brad Zimanek, sports editor of the *Montgomery Advertiser*, quoted defensive back Buddy McClinton as saying, "Connie would come over and say, 'They aren't rushing me. They just peel back and run away every time. I'm telling you, I can run forever.' He just kept on like that."

Late in the fourth quarter, Auburn held a 42-20 lead, with fourth and six on their 16-yard line. Frederick stood back on his 1-yard line. This time when he looked over, Gene gave Frederick the nod.

Auburn Coach "Shug" Jordan was very conservative and took few chances in big games. Frederick knew if he didn't make the first down he would be in the doghouse with Jordan, his teammates, and Auburn fans. He felt he could at least get the first-down yardage and allow the team to run out the clock. Maybe he could make an even bigger play and kill any hope Alabama still had of winning.

McClinton said, "It was the funniest thing when we saw it on film later, because the whole Alabama team was running back to create a wedge. It looked like they were blocking for Connie, as he went the whole way untouched." Two Alabama linemen appeared to run interference for Frederick, who ran right behind them.

Lorendo said later, "Frederick knew Coach Jordan would have his ass if he failed to make the first down. Then he would have my ass."

As the play developed exactly as Frederick had seen on film, Lorendo stood next to Coach Jordan. Jordan looked up and yelled, "Where's the ball? Where's the ball?" Before Lorendo could answer, Frederick came sprinting by.

The last man for Connie to beat was Johnny Musso at the 30-yard line. A nice move took care of him, and Connie was mobbed in the end zone as Auburn fans erupted in wild celebration.

Auburn vs Alabama, Jordan-Hare Stadium, Auburn
November 30, 2013

With one second on the game clock and the score tied 28-28, Chris Davis, Auburn's senior cornerback and punt returner, waited under the goal posts as Alabama attempted to win the game with a fifty-seven-yard field goal. The kick hung in the air, came down short, and landed right in Davis' arms. He started up field, faked right, and swung left.

All Alabama had to do was tackle him or push him out of bounds and the game would head to overtime. Four crushing blocks sprung Davis as he sprinted down the sideline past the Auburn bench, on to the winning touchdown…and forever glory.

Tens of thousands of fans flooded the field, then marched to Toomer's Corner for an all-night celebration of the Play-of-the-Year in the Game-of-the-Year. More importantly, to cheer a historical Iron Bowl victory.

Auburn fans will always remember Chris Davis 109-yard run to destiny in 2013. Those who were around in 1969 will also cherish forever Connie Frederick's eighty-four-yard fake punt.

CHAPTER TWO:

A PHONE CALL FROM SHUG JORDAN

In 1951 Gene Lorendo was finishing his first year on the coaching staff of Presbyterian College in Clinton, South Carolina, where he served as an assistant football coach and head coach of the Blue Hose basketball team. His family—wife, Jane, and two-year-old son, Cam—enjoyed living in Clinton as cherished citizens of the community.

But on a Saturday morning in March, Lorendo received an unexpected phone call that changed the lives of the family. The call was from Ralph "Shug" Jordan, who had been offensive line coach in football and head basketball coach at the University of Georgia when Lorendo was a student-athlete there. Jordan was now the new football coach at Auburn and he wanted Gene to join his staff.

Associated Press release, Clinton, S.C., March 22, 1951:

Presbyterian College assistant coach Gene Lorendo has accepted a position as an assistant coach at Auburn, Athletics Director Walter Johnson announced today. Lorendo leaves Sunday to start spring training in his new job. Lorendo served as both assistant football coach and as head basketball coach at Presbyterian.

The former University of Georgia star led the P.C. Blue Hose basketball team to the Little Four championship in his first year as head coach.

23

LORENDO

In announcing his decision to go to Auburn, Lorendo praised Presbyterian College, its athletic department, and Walter Johnson. "I have thoroughly enjoyed working at Presbyterian and hate to leave," he said. "However, this is an opportunity I cannot afford to turn down at Auburn. In my opinion, Presbyterian College has an ideal athletic plant, one of the best in the South regardless of the size of the school. Both the athletic department and the college administration have given me their full cooperation."

Lorendo's initial salary at Auburn was $5,000 per annum. He received free housing in the Graves Center complex, which he moved into upon his arrival in late March. Jane remained in Clinton as she was eight months pregnant with their second child.

On May 9, 1951, MacLean "Mac" Lorendo was born, and Gene was there for the birth. A week later, the family made the journey from Clinton to Auburn and their new home in Graves Center, a community of cottages that, at the time, housed Auburn's scholarship athletes.

In the springs and falls of the 1950s, students walking across the Auburn campus or in class often heard a booming voice coming from the Drake football practice field east of the stadium. Gene Lorendo, the offensive end coach of the Tigers, was often heard yelling one-liners or cursing at his players. He spewed profanity like a machine gun and yelled constantly. His favorite rebuke was, "If it had been a biscuit, I bet you would have caught it." Or he might have screamed, "You can't catch a cold," to a player after he dropped a pass. To one receiver, an outstanding track sprinter, he yelled, "You might have ten-flat speed, but you have fourteen-flat hands."

One player characterized Lorendo as looking like a real Viking. He stood six-three and weighed 250 pounds. He could have been Paul Bunyan, the mythical giant lumberjack from Minnesota who performed superhuman feats. Lorendo, like Bunyan, hailed from northern Minnesota and both were French Canadian.

Aside from coaching, there was another reason Jordan wanted Lorendo. When Jordan was at the University of Georgia, Coach Wally Butts had a large assistant, Quinton Lumpkin, in charge of the player dorm and dining hall. Coach Lumpkin's responsibility was to maintain control and discipline. When Jordan began to recruit his Auburn staff, the first person he thought of for this similar position was Gene Lorendo. Both Butts and Jordan believed discipline was necessary for a good football team.

On school nights, Lorendo emerged from his Graves Center cottage about thirty minutes before nightly curfew. He sat on the steps and lit his pipe or cigar. Cabin noises, music, conversations, and card games dwindled to whispers by curfew, at which time total silence prevailed.

Tommy Lorino, a star tailback from 1956 to 1958, said Lorendo often caught players coming in after curfew. He filed away the information until the next day when those miscreants were rousted out of bed early to run laps, sprints, or do pushups.

Lorendo also supervised the dining hall. The dietician was "Hoot" Gibson, known for her heavy makeup and even heavier perfume. Jim Dozier, now a retired Delta pilot, was a member of the track team and lived in Graves Center where he waited on tables in the dining hall. Jim said Gibson, a lady in her fifties, was a true character but she, along with her two cooks, Jessie and James, ran an efficient dining facility with plenty of good Southern soul food.

Some athletes made a point of staying in Hoot's good graces. They pampered her with compliments like, "Hoot, you look great today." Her favorites received second helpings of food and desserts. Jimmy "Red" Phillips, an All-American end, admitted to being one of Hoot's pets. Red claimed she made special pies just for him.

At evening meals, Lorendo always tapped on a glass with a metal spoon to get everyone's attention. Players feared he would call on them to give thanks. Paul Susce, a freshman baseball pitcher from Pennsylvania, was one of them. One day Lorendo intoned, "Susce, would you say the blessing for us today?"

Susce, a Catholic, knew only one blessing. "Bless us, O Lord, for the gifts we're about to receive from thy bounty through Christ our Lord." Then he added, "And, Lord, let Auburn win a lot of football games this year." Lorendo loved it, said Susce. "He knew if Auburn won a lot of games that fall, they would be eating good."

Tucker Frederickson, an All-American in the 1960s, said Coach Lorendo had all the players in Graves Center "spooked." The players living in Graves Center loved and admired Lorendo, according to Buck Bradberry, a fellow assistant coach.

According to one former player, if Lorendo thought someone wasn't giving 100 percent, he would be on his ass. His coaching method was old school. He believed in hard work and striving for perfection, whether in practice or in a game.

Red Phillips remembered his dad coming down from Alexander City to watch spring practice one day. Lorendo wasn't pleased with a blocking drill, so he jumped into a three-point stance to demonstrate the proper technique. On the snap, he sprang forward and knocked the defensive tackle backward. Red said his dad never returned for another practice. When asked why, his dad replied, "I've seen enough."

Richard Guthrie, who played for Lorendo from 1958 to 1962 and later became dean of agriculture at Auburn, recalled his days on the field with Lorendo. He remembered Coach yelling and cursing at Mark Helms, himself, and other ends. One day, though, Gene called over a number of seniors and said, "If I've been yelling and cussing at you in past seasons, it is only because you had a chance to help our team."

Gene always pushed his charges to play up to their potential. If he thought someone wasn't giving his all, he was on him every day at practice. Some players hated Lorendo's tactics, but most thrived under him.

CHAPTER THREE:

THE MESABI RANGE

If you asked Gene Lorendo where he was from, he would answer with, "Up on da Range." "Da Range" would be the Mesabi Mountain Range of northeast Minnesota where Eugene Lionel Lorendo was born to Eugene and Katherine Lorendo on December 7, 1921.

Robert Allen Zimmerman, who was also born up on the Mesabi Range, wrote a number of songs about life on the range including the "Girl from the North Country" and "Traveling Down Highway Sixty-One." If you don't recognize the name Robert Zimmerman, maybe you will recognize his stage name—Bob Dylan—and these songs: "Blowing in the Wind" and "The Times They Are A-Changing."

The Mesabi Range is a 125-mile long mountain range of iron ore and mines that runs from Hibbing, Minnesota, to Lake Superior. It is the largest deposit of iron ore in the United States. Mesabi is the Ojibwe Native American tribe's word for "Hidden Giant."

The iron ore was discovered in Hibbing on the western end of the Mesabi Range by Leonidas Merritt and his brothers in 1887, and mining began in 1892. By 1896, there were twenty mines producing three million tons of ore a year. The ore was near the surface so open pit mines were initially established. Later, underground mines were developed.

Before the discovery of iron ore, this area of Minnesota was sparsely populated, and most of the inhabitants made their living in the lumber industry. In the late 1800s, the great forests of Michigan and Minnesota were providing most of the lumber for building the major cities in this part of our country—Chicago, Detroit, Minneapolis/ St. Paul, and Milwaukee.

In the period of 1900 to 1910, a new wave of mining villages started to emerge, resulting in sixty new mines and nine incorporated villages in the Mesabi Range. One of those villages was Gilbert, where Gene Lorendo grew up. Gilbert is located approximately 150 miles north of Minneapolis/ St. Paul, and 90 miles south of International Falls.

The Lorendo family's path to Gilbert began when Gene's French Canadian grandparents, Charles and Adele Bissonnette Laurendeau, migrated to the United States in 1882. The two were married in July 1881 in Saint-Francois-de-Sales, a community on the Saint Lawrence River north of Quebec, Canada. There was an economic depression in Canada at this time and men were seeking jobs to feed their families. Charles Laurendeau found work in the lumber industry of Michigan's Upper Peninsula in the town of Michigamme.

Gene Sr., their first child, was born there on November 30, 1882. Seven more children followed as the Laurendeau family moved on to Lanse, and then settled in Ewen, Michigan. Life was not easy for the Laurendeaus and their eight children, particularly during the long winters of the Upper Peninsula. Just attempting to feed the family, keep warm, and survive the bitter winters was a tremendous challenge.

It was during this time that, for ease of spelling and pronunciation, the Laurendeaus decided to change their name from the French Canadian of their ancestors to a more Americanized version—Lorendo.

In the fall of 1896, just after their last child was born, Charles Lorendo went to work at his job on the evening shift at the local sawmill. He did not return home that night or the next day. Obviously everyone was concerned for his safety. For a week or so, a search was carried out by the local citizens and family in the Ewen community. Charles Lorendo was never found.

Now, with no bread winner, even tougher times faced the Lorendo family. Adele and eight small children ranging in age from three months to fourteen years had no federal or state welfare. They had to survive by taking in washing, cooking baked goods, and doing whatever else they could to earn money. There were a number of French people living in the area, and they pitched in to help the family.

Gene Sr., who was fourteen at the time of his father's disappearance, was now the man of the household and was faced with the tremendous task of feeding and caring for a family of nine. It was said that he was doing a man's work at the age of fifteen. He worked a number of jobs in the lumber industry, starting as a worker in the sawmill, then as a lumberjack in the lumber camps, and finally manning a team of four horses with a large, sturdy wagon hauling logs from the forest to the sawmill.

In March of 1900, Adele married Peter Beaudin. They were able to secure a homestead on a tract of land outside of Ewen in the Bruce Crossing community. Peter and the Lorendo boys pitched in to clear the land and to build a new homeplace. Sometime later, a cousin informed the family that Charles Lorendo was alive and living in Massachusetts. When Adele heard the news, she would only say, "It was the toughest of times."

Gene Sr. continued to live, work, and help support his family in the Ewen area for the next ten years. At the age of twenty-eight and still unmarried, he made the decision to venture out on his own.

News was spreading of the rapidly developing opportunities over in the Mesabi Range of northeastern Minnesota. Gene Sr. was seeking a change in his life and a new opportunity. He had heard the new mining companies were expanding, the area was booming, and they needed lots of men. Also, this portion of northern Minnesota had an abundance of timber in their great forests, and there were a number of jobs available in the lumber industry. After all, this was "Paul Bunyan" country.

It appears Gene Sr. may have been looking for a niche in this booming frontier area and a change from the lumber industry. Working in the lumber industry day after day could be physically exhausting, and after thirteen years in this line of work he may have reached a point in his life where he was ready to do something different.

Lumberjacks hauling logs.

In the small village of Gilbert, Minnesota, activities revolved around the delivery stables where Gene Sr. initially sought work. But within a couple of years, he started a new business as a pioneer drayman, driving a large horse-drawn wagon with detachable sides and hauling heavy loads.

Gilbert was a booming mining village when Gene Sr. arrived in 1910. The village of Gilbert had been a new settlement in 1907-08. A nearby community of Sparta had to be relocated to Gilbert when it was discovered that Sparta had been built over a rich body of iron ore. The original founders of Gilbert made the decision that it would be designed as a planned town, one of very few planned towns in the United States at the time.

The main street would be known as Broadway, and it was designed to be very wide, close to fifty yards from one side of the street to the other. Business buildings such as banks, hardware stores, a doctor's office, the town hall, and the jail would be developed in a specified area with fire-proof buildings. There would be an area set aside for residences, schools, and churches.

On the other end of town was an area designated just for saloons and boarding houses. No other village or townsite on the Mesabi Range was designed in a manner to maintain such proper balance between the different classifications of property.

Main Street, Gilbert, Minnesota

Gilbert became a hustling, bustling community. A number of mines were now operating in the vicinity of Gilbert and there was a huge demand for building materials. A local hardware merchant said his trade in nails was terrific; His firm had sold 100 kegs of nails in a week. These and the many other thriving businesses in the area were ordering new equipment and supplies, most of which came into Gilbert by train. A railroad spur had been built on one end of town. The only problem was how to get these goods and equipment delivered locally. Gene Sr. apparently saw this as an opportunity to start his business as a drayman, delivering everything from houses to furniture to pianos for the saloons, and whatever supplies or equipment the mines needed.

Gene Sr. was described by many local residents as a "big, strong, and powerful man." One of the classic stories in Gilbert of Gene Sr.

was that he picked up a grand piano he was delivering to a saloon and carried it on his back up a flight of stairs to the second floor.

Local youngsters were amazed by watching Gene Sr. tote heavy trunks with one on each shoulder. They were awed by the way he controlled his team of horses with voice commands. He could be standing fifty feet away from his team and they would obey his commands. Gene Sr. was a giant of a man.

At the time there were seven mines just outside of the city limits of Gilbert. In 1908, the town leaders tried to incorporate these mines into the town for the purpose of taxable revenue; however, the Minnesota Supreme Court ruled this action to be illegal, so the town fathers had to find another source of tax dollars. They turned to the largest business sector in the village of Gilbert, the saloons. The population of Gilbert in 1910 was approximately 1,800. There were thirty-two saloons with liquor licenses. The saloon owners were not pleased with the decision for them to pay additional taxes.

Another factor came into play when the Minnesota Legislature passed a law stating a village, town, or city could only have one saloon for every 500 citizens. If this law was enforced, Gilbert could only have three or four saloons. Some of the town officials traveled down to the state capital in St. Paul to ask for an exemption since Gilbert had no other source of taxable income. They were given an exception.

The following paragraph comes from the *Range Reminiscing* newsletter published by the Iron Range Historical Society and provided by the editor, Kathy Bergan.

"There was never such a concentration of different nationalities: French, Germans, Austrians, Poles, Irish, Jews, Slavs, Finns, Swedes, Italians, Greeks, Syrians, and a few Native Americanos. At first their relationships were polite but cool, each keeping to their own activities. With time, the national differences began to fade as each would borrow from each other. They all faced the same challenge. Many felt, they had escaped the frying pan of European slavery into the fire of American capitalist exploitation. Work was hard, hours were long, wages were small, safety measures were

non-existent, and many were killed or maimed for life in the mines."

It was a tough life. The miners worked six days a week with ten-hour workdays. So, when Saturday night came, they were ready to celebrate another week of survival in the mines, and with the hope that they would be back the next Saturday night.

The village of Gilbert was much like the gold and silver mining towns of the Wild West. There was a lot of heavy drinking, fighting, gambling, and brawls on Saturday nights in the saloons of Gilbert. The saloon owners realized they had a serious problem, so they asked the village council for help in handling the problem of the rowdy, drunken miners. The city fathers turned to Gene Sr. for help, hiring him as a constable and the official town bouncer. Gene Lorendo Sr. had found another niche opportunity in Gilbert—removing the disorderly miners from the saloons and streets of Gilbert.

It should be obvious to all why Gene Sr. was chosen for this assignment: Like his son, Gene Jr., he was a giant of a man who had the ability to handle rough and tough situations. Gene Sr. would simply grab the drunken miners by their shirt collars, toss them into his dray, and escort them to their sleeping quarters. He later served as a member of the Gilbert Police Department.

The Mesabi Range was exploding with development and the population of the entire mountain range had reached 55,000 by 1910. There were new steam railroads hauling the iron ore and timber. The ore was loaded on rail cars and taken over to Duluth or Two Harbors, Minnesota, where it was loaded onto ore ships. (Two Harbors is located thirty to forty miles north of Duluth on Lake Superior and was the original home of 3M Company, where I spent thirty-three years in a sales career at 3M.)

These ships then took the ore down to Detroit, Cleveland, Chicago, Erie, and other steel mills on the Great Lakes where the iron ore was smelted into steel. Henry Ford was just getting his Ford Motor Company started down in Detroit, and the availability of steel was a necessity in manufacturing his automobiles.

LORENDO

The Mesabi Railway Company (a trolley) was built and incorporated in 1911 and first operated in 1912. This new trolley service ran from Hibbing to Gilbert, a trip of thirty-five miles that could be made in two hours with stops at Hibbing, Chisholm, Virginia, Eveleth, and Gilbert. We can imagine Gene Sr. taking a two-hour trolley ride down to Hibbing with his lady friend on a Saturday night or Sunday afternoon. Most families did not have an automobile. There were less than 200 miles of paved road in the United States in 1912 and many of the unpaved roads were a challenge.

The new Mesabi Range Trolley on Broadway in 1912.

The state legislature did finally grant towns or villages the right to expand their limits to include the mines and, thus, subject them to taxation. With this source of revenue, the Mesabi Range villages started to rapidly develop new city halls, courthouses, and excellent schools with all the best facilities. Teachers were brought in to the range and provided with living quarters in the villages like Gilbert.

When Gene Sr. arrived in Gilbert, he boarded with the Dubruiel family, which included a daughter named Kathrine. Apparently a romance developed between Gene Sr. and Kathrine, and three years later they were married in September of 1913. The family expanded in June of 1915 when a daughter, Adele, was born. A second daughter, Lorraine, followed in December of 1919. And last but not least, Gene Lorendo Jr. was born December 7, 1921.

CHAPTER FOUR:

THE ORIGIN OF AN ATHLETE:
GENE LORENDO'S EARLY YEARS

We don't know too much about Gene Jr.'s early life. What we do know is that he had the opportunity to attend excellent schools in Gilbert and, at a young age, Gene made the decision he was not going to spend his life digging in the reddish brown dirt of the Mesabi Range as a miner. We also know that Gene loved sports and competition and that, with the melting pot of nationalities in the Gilbert community, Gene had an opportunity to experience a wide range of sporting activities including football, basketball, track, soccer, baseball, softball, cross country skiing, ice skating, hockey, curling, and even croquet.

Yes. Croquet. In August of 1936 a story appeared in the local *Gilbert Herald* newspaper with the headline "Gene Lorendo is Croquet Champ." According to the article, seventy boys participated in croquet matches in four different towns and Gene received a watch for winning first place.

Gene Jr., who one high school classmate recalled as having "beautiful curly red hair," helped his father on a part-time basis and could often be seen riding around town with his father in the dray and, later, in Gene Sr.'s truck. But the young Lorendo was also very involved in school activities. Gilbert was a small school with only 200 students and Gene was a star there. In addition to being an excellent student, Gene Jr. was involved in the orchestra, the school band, the Benzine Club (a science honorary), and the Photo Club.

On the athletic front, Gene sported the Gilbert Warriors' orange and black colors for three of the five sports offered at Gilbert High School: football, basketball, and track. (The other two sports available to students at Gilbert High were swimming and curling; the high school did not play baseball due to the lengthy winters.)

Gene, who was six-foot two-inches tall and weighed 180 pounds, was one of the larger boys on the football, basketball, and track teams. Despite his size, though, Gene's high school football record was not as stellar as his basketball and track performances.

Gene Lorendo Senior Class Picture 1939

In fact, the Gilbert Warriors did not fare well at all during Gene's senior year of football, during which he played end on defense and was a running back on offense for football coach Harold Montgomery. Their team captain and one of their biggest and most talented players, Oliver Oja, was injured with a broken ankle in the fourth game of the seven-game season. The team also suffered a number of injuries to other key players during this tough season, including to their quarterback, Dan Malkovich, and best lineman, Joe Krall.

Gilbert High School Curling Team

LORENDO

The team finished the season with three wins and four losses. In the brief write-ups of the seven games played, there was no record of Gene Lorendo catching a single pass, even though he would later lead the Southeastern Conference in pass receiving at the University of Georgia.

After the senior football season ended, Gene Lorendo and his teammates on the Gilbert football team traveled down to Minneapolis to see their first college football game between the universities of Minnesota and Iowa. As Lorendo observed Iowa and Minnesota do battle on the gridiron, he was told by his coach, Harold Montgomery, that many of the players were on full athletic scholarships.

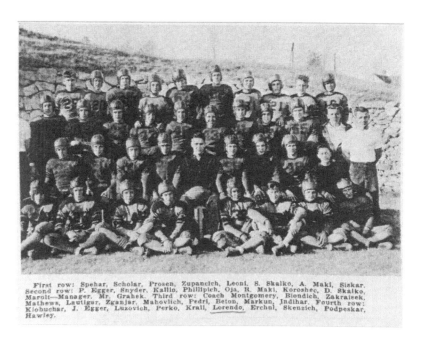

First row: Spehar, Scholar, Prosen, Zupancich, Leoni, S. Skalko, A. Maki, Siskar. Second row: P. Egger, Snyder, Kallio, Phillipich, Oja, R. Maki, Koroshec, D. Skalko, Marolt—Manager, Mr. Grahek. Third row: Coach Montgomery, Biondich, Zakraisek, Mathews, Lautigor, Zganjar, Mahovlich, Pedri, Beton, Markun, Indihar. Fourth row: Klobuchar, J. Egger, Luzovich, Perko, Krall, Lorendo, Erchul, Skenzich, Podpeskar, Hawley.

Gilbert High School Football Team 1938.

Lorendo knew full well that his parents did not have the financial means for him to attend college. Neither of his older sisters had been able to attend college. If he was to obtain a college degree, he had to find a way to get over this hurdle in his life and watching this game got Gene thinking about the possibilities of how he might use his own athletic abilities to secure a college education and reach his goal of becoming a high school coach. For the first time, Gene Lorendo saw an opportunity and a path towards his dream of being a coach.

Football was not the favorite sport at Gilbert High School during this time, perhaps because the games were played at night under the lights and, as winter crept into northern Minnesota, frigid nights did not make watching high school football much fun. Maybe this is why they played a seven-game schedule. Or it could have been there were only seven teams in this area of Minnesota.

Gilbert High School, built in 1911.

Basketball, on the other hand, *was* the favorite sport of the students and the town folks in Gilbert. It was also the favorite sport of Gene Lorendo Jr.

Gilbert had a reputation for producing excellent basketball teams and the 1938-39 team was no exception. Coach Harold Montgomery, who changed coaching hats from football to basketball as the sport seasons changed, molded together another strong team for Gene's senior year of high school play—a team that would go on to win nine games and lose one.

Gene was a leader on the team and was named captain by Coach Montgomery, but he was not a big scorer. Instead, his assignment as the center was to rebound and to be a "garbage" player under the basket: to grab the rebound and put the ball back up and in the goal. Gene scored most of his points (five points a game) with "put backs" or beating his man down the court on a "snowbird" fast break.

This team had talented players in forward Louis Bozich and guard Oliver Oja, who were both named to the first team All-District team. Lorendo and guard Peter Egger were named to the second team. Gilbert defeated the Chisholm Blue Streaks by a score of 31-30 to win the district tournament. It was a glorious victory for the Gilbert team and its fans: More than 5,000 fans were in attendance for the championship game.

Gilbert High School Basketball Team 1938-39

LORENDO

In 1939, all high school teams in Minnesota were eligible for the big state tournament, in which the winners from each of Minnesota's eight districts competed. After winning the district tournament, Gilbert, though one of the smallest high schools to participate in the tournament, was set to represent their district and all of the Mesabi Range down in the state tournament at the Municipal Auditorium in St. Paul.

To say that the students and citizens of Gilbert were excited and fired up about their team's opportunity to play in the big tournament down in the state capital would be an understatement. The whole town and community were 100 percent in support of this team, and telegrams and best wishes cards poured in to the Gilbert team and their captain, Gene Lorendo.

In the first game of the tournament, with 10,000 fans looking on, Gilbert lost to Minneapolis Marshall by the score of 33 to 25. The Minneapolis team, favored to win the tournament, lost their best player to an ankle injury late in the game, hurting their chances of winning the tournament. Gilbert went on the win the consolation bracket of the tournament with victories over Thief River Falls and Hutchison.

(A side note: Gilbert did finally win the state championship in the 1950-51 season, when seven-footer "Boots" Simonovich scored thirty-five points. Gilbert was again the smallest school in the state tournament. Today, Gilbert High is closed and Gilbert students attend an area high school in nearby Eveleth.)

After basketball season, it was time for Gene to prepare for his third sport at Gilbert—track. Gene was a strong member of the team, specializing in the broad jump, high jump, low hurdles, and the 440-yard relay. (Lorendo set the district record in the broad jump, a record upheld into the 1990s.)

Though he was an exceptionally well-rounded and strong athlete, Lorendo's high school athletic career would not have attracted major college recruiters of today. His football team only won three games, and he averaged only five points a game in basketball. However, especially considering his additional talent as a track athlete, a coach with a keen eye for talent might have seen something here that everyone else missed.

After graduating with sixty-two other classmates from Gilbert High School in May of 1939, Gene began to look at his options for college. Eveleth Junior College was only six miles or so from Gilbert, and many of his classmates would be attending this local junior college. Gene was encouraged to attend Eveleth and participate on the football and basketball teams.

But Gene liked the idea of getting away for college, and when his former Gilbert High School pal and mentor, Louis Barle, suggested Minnesota State Teachers College in Duluth, Minnesota, Gene liked the idea. The state teachers college fit right into his plans and goal of becoming a high school coach.

Louis Barle and his brother, Andrew, were excellent athletes at Gilbert High School and close friends of Gene. Louis, who had graduated from Minnesota State Teachers College in 1939 and was playing with the Detroit Lions in the NFL (Andrew would later play football at the University of Minnesota), put in a good word for Gene with the Minnesota State coaches, and Gene soon signed a scholarship to play football and basketball at the college.

CHAPTER FIVE:

UPPING HIS GAME: LORENDO HONES HIS SKILLS AT MINNESOTA STATE TEACHERS COLLEGE

Like many young people then and today, new high school graduate Gene Lorendo was excited to get away from home and attend college out of town. Having signed a scholarship to play football and basketball for the Minnesota State Teachers College (now University of Minnesota-Duluth) in Duluth, Minnesota, he was going to get to do just that.

Duluth was a two-hour drive and sixty miles away from Gilbert—just the right distance to be away from home and still be able to return on the weekends for some home cooking and to have mother do your laundry. Several of Gene's high school friends from Gilbert and the surrounding community were also attending college in Duluth, which was, and still is, one of the largest port cities of the Great Lakes transporting iron ore, coal, and grain.

Because of Duluth's position on the shores of Lake Superior, the largest freshwater lake in the United States, as well as on the side of Spirit Mountain, it's known for its "air conditioned" temperatures in the summer and its freezing temperatures in the winter. (In 2014 there were sixty days below zero.) It's also known for some notable former residents, such as Bob Dylan, one of America's great songwriters, and the noted author Sinclair Lewis.

The city is no stranger to athletic acclaim, either. Dan Devine, former coach of the Missouri Tigers, Notre Dame, and the Green Bay Packers, is a former Duluth resident, and the University of

LORENDO

Minnesota-Duluth is today a major college in Division II of NCAA college football, winner of the 2011 NCAA Men's Hockey national championship, and their women's hockey team has won five national championships.

Back in 1939, Duluth's Minnesota State Teachers College sports teams were holding a great deal of promise. In a preseason write-up on the football team, Coach Lloyd Peterson stated his 1939 team faced another tough schedule. He went on to say a strong line should enable his backs to go places. Coach Peterson indicated the team would be bolstered by the arrival of three husky signees: Lorendo, Orlaski, and Inforzato. Lorendo was listed on the roster as six feet two inches and 185 pounds.

The team played a seven-game schedule and opened the season with Lorendo starting at end in a 21 to 7 victory over Eveleth Junior College. The green and gold Duluth team was undefeated when it played Superior College on the road in the final game of the season. Duluth led 7-0 late in the fourth quarter. The ball was back on Duluth's own 10-yard line with Gene Lorendo back to punt. Superior sent everyone in an all-out effort to block the punt and successfully blocked the punt, badly injuring Lorendo's ankle on the play.

Superior then scored a touchdown a few plays later. When Superior tried to kick the extra point, the kick was wide. An official came in late and threw a flag calling the Duluth team for off sides. Superior tried the kick a second time, hitting the goal post. No good. The same official threw another late flag. Off sides again. Was it "home cooking?" On the third attempt the kick was good. If the extra point had not been good, Duluth would have had an undefeated season, but even with a tie, it was still a very successful season.

In reviewing the season, Coach Peterson commented that one of the stand-outs for his team was Gene Lorendo, and he was excited about Lorendo's potential for the coming season. But when the Minnesota State Teachers College basketball team started practice in December, things were not looking too good for the team.

As they prepared for the upcoming basketball season, Coach Peterson, who also served as Minnesota State Teachers College's basketball coach, had the jitters. He had placed orders during the summer for new uniforms, shoes, and basketballs, all of which were needed for the coming season. None had been received and the first game was one week away.

In addition, Lorendo was still nursing his injured ankle and was unable to practice, and it appeared he would have to sit out until after the Christmas break. Everything seemed to be going wrong for the season.

In basketball, the one thing you must be able to do is to run. Lorendo had always excelled in this phase of basketball with his track background in running the hurdles and the relays. His ability to high jump in track had helped him in his approach to rebounding. He was also good at blocking out when rebounding. Now he could not run on his bad ankle and time did not seem to be on his side.

Gene had a number of strengths as a basketball player. The weakest part of his game was his outside shooting. In high school he had averaged just five points a game, most of which came from layups and foul shots. Now, sidelined with the injured ankle and unable to practice or play, Gene began to do a self-analysis of his basketball skills. Neither of his high school or college coaches had been able to teach him the basics of shooting the basketball. As he was recovering from his ankle injury he made a personal goal that he was going to learn how to shoot the basketball and become a good outside shooter.

In the 1939-1940 college basketball season, Hank Luisetti of Stanford University in California was the best outside shooter in college basketball. Luisetti, who would today be considered a "pure shooter," had changed the game of basketball with his running one-handed shot. Most of the good outside shooters used the two-handed set shot, but only a few players could master the two-handed set shot. Luisetti's one-handed shot was an offensive weapon and he used it with great success, twice leading the NCAA in scoring and becoming the first college player to score fifty points in a game.

Some were skeptical of Luisetti's shooting ability until Stanford, the Pacific Coast champion, came to Madison Square Garden to take on the No. 1 team in the nation, Long Island University, with the nation's longest winning streak of forty-three games. With 17,000 fans in attendance Luisetti, then a six-two, 185-pound sophomore, scored fifteen points, five long outside shots, and was five-for-five on his foul shots. Stanford won the game 45-31.

After Hank Luisetti's performance in Madison Square Garden (and being in New York City, the media capital of the United States), he became everybody's favorite player and was named the college player of the year. Hank, a two-time All-American, was later enshrined in the Naismith Basketball Hall of Fame. (Luisetti, who served as a naval officer in World War II, contracted spinal meningitis after the war, which ended his basketball career. He never played professional basketball, but today he is recognized as one of the greatest shooters to ever play college basketball and was a legend in his time.)

Gene Lorendo confided to a sports writer that he had viewed a short film clip of Hank Luisetti demonstrating his one-handed shooting technique before a feature movie at the local theatre. Lorendo watched the film closely and took in every detail. He even stayed for the next showing of the film clip just to view the Luisetti shooting technique one more time.

Lorendo then went to the basketball court and shot a couple hundred shots every day. Hank Luisetti was the Larry Bird of his day. He believed if you get the fundamentals down right and you take enough repetitions, you can become a good shooter. Lorendo bought into this program 100 percent and was determined to become a good shooter.

Despite the opportunity his injury provided for Lorendo to work on his shooting skills, though, he was frustrated with his injured ankle and the direction of the basketball program at Minnesota State Teachers College. So, during the Christmas holidays of 1939-40, he made the first of what would be several abrupt decisions in his early life: Gene transferred to Eveleth Junior College in nearby Eveleth, Minnesota.

CHAPTER SIX:

FROM TRAGEDY TO TRIUMPH: LORENDO BLOSSOMS AT EVELETH JUNIOR COLLEGE

When Lorendo made the decision to leave Minnesota State Teachers Junior College in January of 1940 and transfer to Eveleth Junior College, which was located only a few miles from his hometown of Gilbert, he was told that he would be ineligible to participate in any sport for two quarters.

But that did not stop Gene from finding a way to play his favorite sport, basketball.

Many of Lorendo's friends from Gilbert High School were students at Eveleth Junior College and, as Gene's ankle injury slowly healed, he was invited to join an independent amateur basketball team playing out of his hometown, the Gilbert Co-Op Angels. The team was made up of former high school and college players from the local area.

Lorendo was excited to finally get back on the court and be a player on the Gilbert Co-Op team, which won thirty-nine straight games during the time Lorendo was playing for the Angels. The team played in an industrial league up on the Mesabi Range and in tournaments all over Minnesota and Wisconsin—wherever there was a team that wanted to play basketball, the Gilbert Co-Op Angels were ready to accept the challenge.

Playing for the Gilbert Co-Op out of his hometown gave Lorendo a unique opportunity to work on the new one-handed push shot he had adopted from Hank Luisetti. The team was winning most of their games by twenty to thirty points, so if Lorendo missed one or two of his long shots it was no big deal. He was having fun as a student at Eveleth Junior College, where he was playing his favorite sport and concentrating on his goal of becoming a good outside shooter and a more complete basketball player. And Lorendo was making steady progress with his shooting while having an excellent season as one of Gilbert Co-op's leading scorers.

On March 2, 1940, Lorendo was traveling with the Gilbert Co-Op team down to Minneapolis to participate in a basketball tournament when the station wagon he and several of his teammates were riding in was involved in a head-on collision. Their driver was killed and several of the players were injured, including Lorendo, who suffered a back injury that caused him to drop out of school at Eveleth Junior College while he recovered.

By the next fall, though, Lorendo had partially recovered from his back injury and was rounding back into football shape. He was excited and looking forward to the coming (1940) football season at Eveleth Junior College. The Eveleth team went on to win the Minnesota Junior College football championship that year, but during the season, Lorendo reinjured his back and had to undergo surgery in nearby Virginia, Minnesota, after the season.

Gene Lorendo was a popular figure at Eveleth Junior College. He received a twenty-foot long letter with nearly 100 individual handwritten notes from classmates, which was personally delivered to Gene in the hospital by Eveleth's head football coach, Jack Malevich.

At this point in Lorendo's life, his career as an athlete was in jeopardy. He had experienced two tough injuries in the last year and he faced the challenge of physical therapy and getting back into top playing condition. But what happened next is a most unusual sports story, an exciting and generally unknown part of Gene Lorendo's athletic career—Lorendo not only recovered from his injuries and surgeries, his athletic accomplishments in football, basketball, and track simply took off like a rocket. In a two-year period, he blossomed from being a no-star player to what would

A LETTER TO LORENDO

Gene Lorendo, versatile Gilbert athlete attending Eveleth Junior college, is in municipal hospital in Virginia recuperating from a minor operation for an injury suffered in an auto accident some time ago. Eveleth students got together to send Gene a letter, and before they all got through writing their little notes to the 3-letter athlete, it turned out to be 20-ft. letter with nearly 100 notes. Coach Jack Malevich de-livered the letter to him Tuesday night— and it will probably take him the rest of the week to read everything on it. Pictured here are Butch Granross, at the top of the step ladder, Pierre Mattei, left, and Sergio Gambucci, right, teammates of Lorendo's on the 1940 NJCC football championship eleven, and two co-eds, giving the letter a once-over before rolling it up. The girls are Carol Differ-ding and Alberta Kuzma.

Letter to Gene Lorendo from the students at Eveleth Junior College. Lorendo was recovering from surgery for a back injury suffered in an auto accident.

today be considered a five-star player in football, basketball, and track.

During the 1940-41 season, the Eveleth Junior College basketball team played an exhibition game against a Chinese All Star Team. This Chinese team had upset a number of college teams in their tour of the United States by applying a full-court press against their opponents. The Chinese team only had one player who was over six feet tall, but they used four guards on the floor pressing their opponents the full length of the court. This tactic worked very well at the start of the game as the Chinese team jumped out to a 6-2 lead.

Eveleth Coach Jack Malevich called a timeout and instructed his players: Four of them were to bring the ball up the court while Lorendo stationed himself at the top of the foul circle on the other end of the court. The remaining four Eveleth players were told to get the ball up the court and then to Lorendo. After Lorendo scored three times in a row, the Chinese coach called a timeout and took off the full-court press. Eveleth won 61-49 with Lorendo scoring eighteen points.

Eveleth Junior College Basketball Team

LORENDO

In the 1940-41 basketball season for the Eveleth Tigers, Lorendo led the team to thirteen victories and the Northern Junior College Championship. Their only loss that year was to one of their biggest rivals, the Hibbing Cardinals, which Eveleth later defeated in a rematch game, gaining sweet revenge on their home court.

Gene averaged thirteen points a game as he mastered the art of outside shooting on the basketball court. As one writer stated, Lorendo stormed into the conference demonstrating the art of outside shot-making. Many of Lorendo's points were long field goals, scored as three points today. One writer stated that, as the season progressed, the Eveleth team, paced by Gene Lorendo, gained momentum and rolled over its opponents. He stated Lorendo was easily the most outstanding player in the conference.

Lorendo running the high hurdles at Eveleth Junior College in 1942.

LORENDO

When the successful basketball season was over, Lorendo moved on to the track season. In a meet with Eveleth's archrival Hibbing, Lorendo stole the show by scoring twenty-three points with the following performance: first in the 120-yard hurdles; first in the high jump; second in the shot put; first in the 220 low hurdles; and first in the broad jump. He also ran on the winning relay team. Later he scored twenty-six points in a triangular meet with Itasca and Duluth junior colleges. The Eveleth terror compiled this amazing total by either winning or placing in seven events.

In the Minnesota Junior College Conference annual track meet, Lorendo scored twenty-four points and set three new conference records: In the broad jump he leaped twenty-three feet two inches; in the high jump he cleared the bar at six feet three inches; and in the 120-yard high hurdles he ran 15.5 seconds. He also won the 220-yard hurdles; placed third in the shot put, and won a second place on a relay team. One writer described Lorendo's effort as "Superman."

The 1941 football team had only four returning lettermen and a total of twenty players, but the orange and blue Eveleth Junior College team won another conference championship. The football team would go undefeated in the 1941 season.

Eveleth Junior College Football Team 1941

Leading the offense was an All-Conference quarterback, Sergio Gambucci. Lorendo was one of the key players on the team—an All-Conference fullback and an outstanding end on defense. The team featured a strong defense that allowed only two touchdowns during the entire season and the offense averaged twenty-three points a game. In the biggest game of the year against Itasca Junior College, Lorendo came through with a big play in the fourth quarter when he blocked a punt and a teammate recovered it in the end zone for a safety. Eveleth won this hard-fought game by the score of 8-6, then finished off their undefeated 1941 season with a 52-0 win over Hibbing.

Needless to say, Lorendo was attracting quite a bit of attention and his name was being mentioned as one of the top athletes in the state of Minnesota. Recruiting rumors were flying about where Lorendo would sign a scholarship. Tom Lieb, head football coach of the Florida Gators, was up in Minnesota on a recruiting trip and Lieb, a former Notre Dame tackle in the days of Knute Rockne, expressed strong interest in Lorendo signing with the Gators.

One sportswriter commented in his "Scoop Department" that Lorendo and Louis Bozichof of the Eveleth Junior College football team would sign with Colorado in a few days. The University of Minnesota, a strong football power at this time, expressed strong interest in signing Lorendo, too, and sent their coaches up to Eveleth several times during the season to see him play.

As Lorendo was basking in the attention and celebrating his twentieth birthday with several of his close friends on December 7, 1941, they received the shocking news that Pearl Harbor had been attacked by the Japanese. Though this did not immediately affect Lorendo, it would soon prove to be a big factor in his life and the path of his career.

Despite this horrible news, everyone at Eveleth was excited about the coming basketball season after the previous stellar 1940-41 season. Coach Malevich scheduled a special exhibition game with the House of David team to kick off the season. The House of David team was a bearded Israelite basketball team that played the Globetrotters throughout the United States and Europe during the 1930s, '40s, and '50s.

A second exhibition game was played against the All American Red Heads, the first women's professional basketball team in the USA. The famous Red Heads—all the team members dyed their hair red—was a "barnstorming" team from Iowa. The game was a smashing success with the fans.

Lorendo and his teammates at Eveleth went on to win the conference basketball championship again in the 1941-42 season, with Lorendo leading the conference in scoring while averaging eighteen points a game.

LORENDO'S MEDIA STAR SHINES

In addition to his athletic prowess, the sports media began discovering and revealing another side to Lorendo—his literary talents. A number of area sport writers referred to Gene as the "Poetic" Lorendo (an example of his poetry will be found later in the book). Bernard Swanson, a writer in the Twin Cities with the *St. Paul Pioneer,* wrote the following feature story on Gene Lorendo in the spring of 1942.

One-Man Gang Lorendo...Eveleth's Best Gem "Combines Poetic Mind, Meter"

Remember that poetic gem about "Full many a flower is born to blush unseen, and waste its sweetness on the desert air"?

Well...Gene Lorendo may not be a posy, and Eveleth can't exactly be considered a desert in these days of wartime emphasis on metal and metallurgy.

But hidden away in a home on the Range is a young man who combines the important features of poetic mind and meter. He is Jack Malevich's most fragrant bloom at Eveleth Junior College. All and sundry will tell you he is one of the most lethal one-man gangs that has cavorted in the Iron Range pasturage.

This past winter, for instance, Lorendo mustered a paltry total of 294 points in sixteen conference basketball games, for an average of eighteen points a game. In one game alone, he fluttered the nets for thirty-seven points, on sixteen field goals and five free throws, to break the previous record of twenty-nine points. With a remarkably coordinated one-hand push shot as his scoring weapon, and the story goes that he learned it by studying a movie short in which Hank Luisetti, the Stanford phantom, demonstrated it.

In football he was second in the conference in scoring and was a monotonous selection for All-Conference fullback. And he never did care much about football.

In track he was the leading scorer in the annual conference track meet where he displayed his versatility in winning a number of events and breaking three conference records.

He stands six feet two, weighs 185 pounds and is twenty years old. Graduating from Eveleth Junior College in June, he is just growing up and has two more years of collegiate competition ahead of him, wherever he elects to finish his education.

His No.1 fan of his brilliant career is his sister Lorraine living in St. Paul. She faithfully jingles the sports department after each athletic contest with the same breathless question and hope: "How did my kid brother do tonight?"

Another sportswriter wrote of Lorendo:

While it is difficult to single out an individual for special mention on a championship squad as being directly responsible for the team's success, one can't ignore the fact that Gene Lorendo has been an important cog in the athletic machine which has brought three consecutive titles to Eveleth Junior College. Lorendo, who established an outstanding athletic record at Gilbert High School, stormed into the junior college conference last year to demonstrate the real art of shot making on the basketball court. He earned All-Conference honors by averaging eighteen points a game. In track competition, Lorendo, who stands six-two, distinguished himself as the number one-cinder track performer in the conference, taking first place in the high jump, broad jump, and the hurdles in every meet. In five of the track meets he scored over twenty points. As a 185-pound fullback for the Eveleth Tigers he played an important part in the team's march to the conference championship. He was second in the league in scoring. "He was an ace in three collegiate sports...that's Eveleth's Gene Lorendo."

As speculation grew in the press, and no doubt in coffee shops and barber shops around the Mesabi Range and beyond, about just where their local athletic wonder would head for the rest of his college career, Gene pulled another surprise. He chose an unlikely school.

CHAPTER SEVEN:

HOW DID LORENDO END UP AT THE UNIVERSITY OF GEORGIA? WHAT WAS THE MISSING LINK?

In the summer of 1942, Gene Lorendo was flying high. He had just completed two great years at Eveleth Junior College in northern Minnesota, and Eveleth had finished the year as the dominate junior college in state sports, winning the junior college championships in football, basketball, and track.

Gene Lorendo had been an All-Star player on the football team and the MVP of all the ten junior college basketball teams in the state. Plus, he was the most valuable performer in the Minnesota Junior College annual track meet.

His stock had risen from an unknown player to one of the top prospects in that part of the country in both football and basketball. (Lorendo would have been a five-star football and basketball prospect in today's recruiting lingo.) Newspapers were speculating about where he might sign a scholarship. Wisconsin? Florida? Iowa? Colorado? Minnesota? Georgia?

Lorendo ended up picking what seemed to be the least likely option—he signed to play for the University of Georgia 1,100 miles south of his hometown in Minnesota. Why, of all places, would he choose Georgia? It was a question that kept prickling in my mind as I did research on this book. What **was** the link between Lorendo and the University of Georgia?

I had the answer in my hands at one point when I dropped the ball.   One day while having lunch with Lorendo (before I made the decision to write this book) I asked him, "How did you end up down at Georgia?"

In the forties, it was common knowledge that Coach Wally Butts of Georgia was one of the best recruiters in college football. But a highly rated football and basketball prospect from northern Minnesota, more than 1,000 miles to the north, was a stretch even for Coach Butts.

As I remembered back to that conversation with Coach Lorendo, I recalled that he told me he was recruited by a coach on the Georgia coaching staff. Lorendo also mentioned to me that a Georgia alum and a geologist, who was an executive with a local mining company, was very interested in having him sign with Georgia.

What I think could have taken place: The Georgia alum, who was possibly a recruiter, or "bird dog," for the Georgia football program, could have given Coach Butts a scouting report on Lorendo, telling him that Lorendo was a big athlete with excellent speed who was a track star in high jumps and hurdles, an All-Junior college player in football at fullback and end, as well as being a tremendous basketball player with good hands. Coach Butts no doubt could have visualized him as an outstanding athlete and a potential star football player.

In a later conversation, Gene's son, Mac, also told me that his dad was initially recruited to play basketball at Georgia. While doing research for this book, I came across a newspaper story from a northern Minnesota paper that mentioned Coach Elmer Lampe was in town to see Eveleth Junior College play a basketball game.

I was not familiar with the names of the Georgia coaching staff in those days and I had never heard of Coach Elmer Lampe, but I found out that he was the head basketball coach and assistant football coach at the University of Georgia from 1938 to 1946.

According to the article, Lampe was in town on a recruiting trip. More specifically, Coach Lampe's main purpose for the visit was to see Gene Lorendo, who was leading all of the Minnesota junior colleges in scoring play. As Georgia's head basketball coach in

1942, he would likely have known about the outstanding play of Lorendo, the MVP of all the Minnesota junior colleges.

But Lampe had another connection that probably led him to the Mesabi Range that year. Eveleth was Lampe's hometown and he still had a lot of friends there, including the coaches at Eveleth Junior College. He had no doubt heard a lot about Lorendo before he arrived, and he apparently was a pretty darn good recruiter—he had, after all, married the daughter of a former Minnesota governor—so he was up to the challenge of recruiting Gene Lorendo.

Though Lampe was interested in Lorendo as a basketball player (it should be noted that Gene's personal goal was to play college basketball since it was his favorite sport), football was king at Georgia during this time period. If Georgia's head football coach, Wally Butts, wanted you to play football, everything else was secondary, and Butts probably had Lorendo on his radar screen.

Coach Butts had a reputation for recruiting outstanding players from the northern states. He had recruited a number of the top players in the country from Ohio and Pennsylvania: Charley Trippi, Georgia's All-American back, was from Pennsylvania and Frank Sinkwich, another All-American back, was from Ohio. (Both players are in the College Football Hall of Fame.)

Lorendo, at six-two and 185 pounds, was one of the bigger players of the '40s who also possessed rare athletic abilities. Butts, who had an eye for talent (Butts was known for recruiting quality athletes and then determining how the player could fit into his innovative offense), probably saw in Lorendo a great athlete with a lot of upside potential as a football player, and invited Lorendo to come down to Athens for the summer of '42 to work out with the football team—an opportunity for Butts and his staff to evaluate the talents of Gene Lorendo.

Lorendo spent all summer down in Athens working out in the heat and humidity of the South with the Georgia team. I am not sure what happened next with Gene Lorendo. What I do know is that he left the Georgia team in late August just as fall practice was getting started.

LORENDO

Lorendo could have been concerned that he would not get much playing time on this talented Georgia team since he was a running back at the time and Georgia had two great All-American backs in Sinkwich and Trippi, as well as a strong supporting cast of players including "Rabbit" Smith, Johnny Rauch, George Poscher, and Van Davis.

It may simply have been that Gene hated the heat and humidity of the South, though another reason—and the reason that has been most publicized—was that Gene left the team to join the service. The United States was in the middle of World War II and men everywhere were being drafted or joining the military. When I attended the memorial service for Coach Lorendo at the Presbyterian Church of the Hills in John's Creek, Georgia, the printed program stated he attended the University of Georgia in the summer of 1942 and left to join the Coast Guard.

Whatever the reason, after working out with the Georgia team all summer and a few days of fall practice, Lorendo slipped out of Athens on the Saturday night train to Atlanta.

That decision cost Gene an opportunity to play for a remarkable Georgia team. The Bulldogs were undefeated and ranked No. 1 in the country in '42, when an unranked Auburn team broke the hearts of the Georgia faithful. Monk Gafford and his War Eagle teammates upset Georgia by a score of 27-14 in Columbus, Georgia, though the Bulldogs went on to defeat Georgia Tech, the No. 2 team in the country and their in-state rival, to finish the season ranked No. 3 nationally.

At the end of the college football season, Ohio State was named the No. 1 team in the country. (Their coach was Paul Brown, who would later be the outstanding coach of the Cleveland Browns.) Fred Sinkwich won the Heisman award that year, and Georgia received a bid to play UCLA in the Rose Bowl. The Georgia Bulldogs defeated UCLA 9- 0 to cap off a great season.

Lorendo had missed out on an opportunity to be a member of the 1942 Georgia Bulldogs SEC championship team and to play in the Rose Bowl.

CHAPTER EIGHT:

A BRIEF STINT AT IOWA STATE TEACHER'S COLLEGE

In August of 1942, when Gene Lorendo left Athens, Georgia, and the University of Georgia football team, the stated reason given for his departure was that he was going to enlist in the military. Thousands of young men were being drafted or were enlisting in the service. We were in the middle of World War II with Germany and Japan. The build-up of our armed forces was affecting the lives of all the young men throughout our country.

But one day when I was googling Gene Lorendo on the Internet, up popped a newspaper story dated September 1942 about Gene Lorendo scoring the winning touchdown at Iowa State Teachers College (now Northern Iowa University) in Cedar Falls, Iowa. This college was a member of the North Central Football Conference in '42 along with Augustana, South Dakota University, North Dakota University, South Dakota State, North Dakota State, Drake, and Omaha University.

(About this same time, an article appeared in a Minnesota newspaper stating that Lorendo had left the University of Georgia and had enrolled at the University of Iowa. Someone apparently had received word that Gene was now attending college in Iowa and they may have assumed he was in Ames at the University of Iowa.)

The Northern Iowa sports information office confirmed Gene Lorendo had played at the Iowa State Teachers College in 1942. He was a star running back on the team and was listed on the roster as six-foot two-inches and 185 pounds. One preseason article from the school newspaper said that Coach "Buck" Starbeck was excited about his backfield that year with his All-Star fullback back healthy after being injured the previous season.

And he was likewise pleased with Gene Lorendo, who had an uncanny ability to shake off tacklers as he ran inside or outside on sweeps. Coach Starbeck said in the article that he had high expectations for his team and Lorendo as the season approached. Gene's hometown was listed as Gilbert, Minnesota. (One story listed his nickname as "Frenchy," a nod to Lorendo's French Canadian roots.)

The basketball coach at Iowa State Teachers College was quoted in the school's newspaper as saying he was looking forward to Lorendo joining the basketball team for the coming season as well. He was very much aware of Lorendo's outstanding play at Eveleth Junior College up in northern Minnesota.

Yet another newspaper story reported that a new football star had emerged for the Iowa State Teachers College Panthers. He was Gene Lorendo, a star running back. In one of the toughest conference games in years, the Panthers had defeated the North Dakota Bisons 27-19 in their first game of the season. The star of the day was Gene Lorendo, who ran for two touchdowns, intercepted a pass, and kicked three extra points. In a game against the South Dakota State Jackrabbits, Lorendo was the leading ground gainer in the game. One writer said of Lorendo: "Gene swivel-hipped down the field twisting and turning out of the reach of would-be tacklers for two touchdowns."

Then a totally unexpected development took place. After the fifth game of the season with South Dakota University, Lorendo shocked everyone by leaving the team. Coach Starbeck was very upset to learn his star running back had left school to join the Coast Guard.

CHAPTER NINE:

A PRE-SERVICE DETOUR TO THE NATIONAL BASKETBALL LEAGUE

Gene Lorendo left the Iowa State Teachers College football team in November of 1942 and enlisted in the U.S. Coast Guard. He signed the papers for enlistment in Minneapolis, Minnesota, on November 5, 1942. There was a massive build-up of the armed forces during this time, with a major military campaign in Europe fighting to stop Hitler and his German war machine. The United States was still recovering from the attack on Pearl Harbor by the Japanese on December 7, 1941 (Gene's twentieth birthday). Japan was continuing their plan to invade, expand, and overrun the islands of the Pacific.

Gene was twenty years old when completing his papers for enlistment. He listed his civilian occupation as "athlete." Most of the references he gave when applying for the Coast Guard were former coaches from high school, junior college, and Iowa State Teachers College.

His former Iowa State Teachers College football coach, Clyde "Buck" Starbeck, remarked that, "Lorendo was a good man, but he needed to finish whatever he started," referring to the fact that Lorendo, his star running back, had left the team in the middle of the season.

In the fall of 1942, the U.S. military services had a large backlog of men who had been drafted or had volunteered to serve our country. For this reason, Gene was placed in the inactive reserves until an opening was available for his basic training in the Coast Guard.

LORENDO

In researching the decisions made by Lorendo during this period in his life, one wonders why he left the Iowa State Teachers College football team in the middle of the season when he was having a great year as their star football player. Did he want to join the war effort and help our country defeat Germany and Japan? Maybe. Maybe not. The next development in Lorendo's life made the situation even more complicated.

Several newspapers announced in early December of 1942 that Gene Lorendo had signed a contract to play professional basketball for the Oshkosh All Stars of Oshkosh, Wisconsin. The Oshkosh All Stars were the 1941-42 defending champions of the National Basketball League. This team had won five straight championships and was a dynasty in the late thirties and early forties, much like the Boston Celtics and the Los Angeles Lakers would be in more recent times.

The National Basketball League (NBL) was the predecessor to the NBA (National Basketball Association). The NBL was a professional basketball league created by three large corporations—General Electric, Firestone, and Goodyear—and comprised mainly of teams from the Great Lakes region. Five current NBA teams trace their history to the National Basketball League: The Los Angeles Lakers (then the Minneapolis Lakers), the Sacramento Kings (then the Rochester Royals), the Atlanta Hawks (then the Tri Cities Blackhawks), the Philadelphia 76'ers (then the Syracuse Nationals), and the Detroit Pistons.

This sudden turn of events in Lorendo's life can probably be traced to an earlier relationship in his life. One of Gene's best friends and mentor from high school was Louis Barle, an outstanding athlete who had starred at Gilbert High School in both football and basketball. Barle had attended the Minnesota State Teachers College in Duluth where he continued his career as a star player in both sports. Lorendo had followed Barle to the Minnesota State Teachers College, where he played football and had planned to play basketball until a football injury prevented him from playing.

After college, Louis Barle had signed by the Detroit Lions of the NFL as a defensive back and punter. At the end of the football season, though, he agreed to play professional basketball for the Oshkosh All Stars where he became an All-Star player in the National Basketball League. He possessed excellent ball-handling skills and was one of the best outside shooters in the league.

Barle was drafted by the military in October of 1942. Knowing the Oshkosh All Stars needed players to replace those entering the service, Barle knew first-hand of Lorendo's basketball skills and most likely suggested to the Oshkosh team that they take a look at his Gilbert teammate and buddy, Gene Lorendo. Someone, either Louis Barle or representative of the Oshkosh All Stars, contacted Gene while he was at Iowa State Teachers College to gauge his interest in joining this professional basketball team.

Lorendo, though a star college football player, made the decision to leave the Iowa State Teachers College team in the middle of the season to join the Oshkosh All Stars. He was excited about the opportunity to sign and play professional basketball. Not just for any team, but the defending champion of the National Basketball League, the Oshkosh All Stars. The All Stars were the dominant team of the NBL. This was an once-in-a-lifetime opportunity for Lorendo to play professional basketball, his favorite sport, and he was excited about the opportunity to play in what was the NBA of the 1940s.

The Oshkosh All Stars were then led by a rugged six-four center by the name of Leroy "Cowboy" Edwards. Edwards had a deadly hook shot and an array of moves around the goal. All-American Edwards had played two years at Kentucky before signing a contract for $2,400 a season. Adolph Rupp, the great Kentucky coach, did not blame his young star for signing with the NBL since Rupp himself was only making $2,800 a year. The second star on the team was forward Connie Mack Berry, who had played college basketball at North Carolina State. Berry, an all-round athlete, also played professional football in the NFL and major league baseball with the White Sox in the American League.

One of the sportswriters who covered the Oshkosh team wrote that the team was very thin at the forward position after losing three top players to the military draft. Louis Barle was one of those talented players who was missed, along with Herb Witasek and

Bob Carpenter. Lorendo was signed as a forward to help shore up their rebounding. He was a key player off the bench during the 1942-43 season.

The league was struggling as they continued to lose players to the war. George Halas, owner of the Chicago Bears NFL team and Chicago's NBL team, decided to fold his team. The league was still able to field a Chicago franchise thanks to the local Studebaker plant, which had been converted to a war-industry production plant, so a number of the Chicago team players were employed in the plant and became exempt from the draft.

Several of the Harlem Globetrotters were able to join the Chicago team after getting jobs in the Studebaker plant. This was the first integrated team in the National Basketball League and in professional basketball as it slowly developed into one of the strongest teams in the league.

Other noteworthy players who played in the National Basketball League were George Mikan, the first big man in college basketball at DePaul University and later a star with the Minneapolis Lakers; Dolph Schayes, a great forward with the Syracuse Nationals; Otto Graham, the former Cleveland Browns All-Pro and NFL quarterback, and Chuck Connors of "The Rifleman" of television show fame and a former Los Angeles Dodgers first baseman.

CHAPTER TEN:

HEADING OFF
TO THE COAST GUARD

On January 31 of 1943, Gene reported for active duty at Omaha, Nebraska. From Omaha he traveled by train to the Brooklyn Naval Yard for his basic training, where he received vigorous physical training in all phases of Coast Guard duty.

One of his instructors was Jack Dempsey, who was the heavyweight champion of the world from 1919-1926 and one of the most popular boxers of his time. The Associated Press had voted Dempsey as the greatest fighter in the past fifty years. Dempsey had volunteered for national service after the attack on Pearl Harbor and was commissioned as a commander in the Coast Guard. He pushed his men in training to their physical limits, reminding them they had to be in top shape to accomplish their duties in the Coast Guard.

While Gene was completing his training, he received word that his sister, Lorraine, had enlisted in the Navy's Waves. After completing basic training Lorraine was ordered to duty in Texas and later served in Hawaii.

Gene completed his basic training in April of 1943 and was assigned to the Cleveland Coast Guard Station. He worked there as a Coast Guardsman on Lake Erie, Lake Huron, and up to Sault Ste. Marie, Canada. Lorendo managed to get into some sort of trouble, which resulted in him being transferred in November of 1943 to the Duluth (Minnesota) Coast Guard Station on Lake Superior, a good situation for Gene. He was now stationed only sixty miles from his hometown of Gilbert, so he was able to enjoy weekends and home-cooked meals with his family.

LORENDO

Everything was going along great for Gene until the end of the basketball season. He was living in the old Cascade Hotel in Duluth and enjoying life to its fullest under war-time conditions. As one of his Coast Guard friends said, "Lorendo had it made." Gene was utilizing his basketball skills playing on both the Duluth Coast Guard team as well as a local team, the Butler Shipyards.

These teams were in two different leagues and Gene was the best player on both teams. At the end of the season it was decided the winner of each league would meet in a championship game. The Butler Shipyard team was paying Lorendo $20 a game to play for them, so he made the decision to play for the Butler Shipyard team in the big championship game against his own Coast Guard team. The Butler Shipyard team won the game decisively. That decision turned out to have major consequences for Lorendo.

The commander of the Coast Guard unit in Duluth was furious. The next week Gene received orders that he was being transferred to the North Superior Station, located approximately 100 miles north of Duluth in Grand Marais, Minnesota. The Coast Guard commander, Captain Ford, supposedly said to Lorendo, "You won't even see a damn basketball where you are being assigned."

The North Superior Station, located just south of the Canadian border in the "boondocks," was obviously not the assignment most desired by Coast Guard personnel. North Superior was right in the middle of the arctic front that includes International Falls and the rest of Minnesota as well as Wisconsin and Michigan. Winters there are long and extremely cold, and the biting wind off Lake Superior goes right through you.

Gene, who arrived at the North Superior Station in the middle of a freezing blizzard, was not very happy with his time there so, as another winter was approaching in the fall of 1944, he developed a strategy to get out. He started telling his superiors that he joined the service to help win the war. He stated that he had not seen a single German or Japanese during his duty in North Superior; the only people he had seen were fishermen. Lorendo said he was ready for some action.

We have all heard the story to be careful what you ask for or you might just get it. A short time later, Gene received orders to report to Alameda Coast Guard Training Station in San Francisco, California. He had time for one last trip back to his hometown of Gilbert. After spending a few days with his family and enjoying some good home cooking, it was time for him to leave for San Francisco and say goodbye to his friends and family.

The day after he departed from his hometown of Gilbert, an article appeared in the Gilbert Herald. It is thought Gene's mother wrote this comment: "Why is it that the real unsung heroes of this war are the ten million mothers of twenty million boys? If guns, hate, and ammunition constitute a war, what term is used to define patience, love, and courage?"

The newspaper article went on to say:

"Today, we saw a parting between a young Coast Guardsman and his mother. He was feeling bad about it all, but she was all assurance and courage. She was smiling at him as he mounted the steps of the bus, but we could see that her heart was breaking. Still, she smiled. This is not mentioned as an uncommon occurrence. It is happening every day, in every hour throughout our country. So, we fight with twenty-million-strong-soldiers and ten million mothers."

Gene traveled most of the way to California by train. In route he met another member of the Coast Guard in St. Louis named Jimmy Babb. Babb was from Kentucky and had played college basketball, so he and Gene had two things in common—the Coast Guard and basketball—and they developed an immediate friendship.

They arrived at Alameda Coast Guard Training Station on November 2, 1944, and departed by ship for Hawaii on November 14. Their ship docked at Pearl Harbor on November 23. Gene Lorendo celebrated his twenty-third birthday on December 7 in Hawaii, exactly three years after the attack on Pearl Harbor. On December 13, they boarded a Landing Ship Tank (LST 789) at Pearl Harbor.

The LST is a vessel that supports amphibious operations by carrying vehicles, cargo, and troops. LST 789 had been built in

Pittsburgh, Pennsylvania, and was commissioned on September 11, 1944—she was 327 feet 9 inches long (longer than a football field), had a beam (or width) of 50 feet, and her top speed was 11.6 knots (11.6 nautical miles per hour or approximately 13 miles per hour at top speed). The men on LST 789 joked that LST stood for "Large Slow Target."

Her crew consisted of eight officers and 104 enlisted men armed with two 50-caliber and four 30-caliber machine guns, plus seven 40-mm guns and six 20-mm guns as well as small arms including rifles and pistols.

After leaving Pennsylvania, LST 789 traveled down the Ohio and Mississippi rivers to New Orleans. Next was a shakedown cruise in the Gulf of Mexico, before being loaded with heavy equipment, and then departing for Hawaii by way of the Panama Canal. After arriving in Hawaii, the crew spent the next two months on logistics and training maneuvers, including a dress rehearsal on the island of Maui for the assault on Iwo Jima.

It was the best of times, training each day in the paradise-like islands and enjoying beautiful Hawaii in their time off. But soon the crew realized the task that lay ahead of them: to attack and invade the heavily fortified island of Iwo Jima.

Marion Gilbert, now a retired Bell South executive from Macon, Georgia, had made the trip with LST 789 from Pittsburgh to Hawaii. Marion was a radar operator and he and Gene hit it off right away. With Gene being from Gilbert, Minnesota, and Marion's last name being Gilbert, they had something in common besides just being shipmates on LST 789.

Marion, who is today the last surviving member of the 112-man LST 789 crew, said that during this time in Hawaii and after they were underway to Iwo Jima, the men of LST 789 played a lot of basketball. Any time a unit would play them, they accepted the challenge. The LST had a basketball goal on the ship. When they arrived in a new port, a basketball court could usually be found wherever American military personnel were stationed.

According to Marion, Gene was the star of their team and Jimmy Babb was an outstanding player. Marion stated they played some really good teams and he didn't remember them losing a single game. In one tough game, an opposing player was roughing up Jimmy Babb. Gene called a time out, went over to the opposing player, and said, "If you do that again, I will kick your ass." Marion said the opposing player never touched Babb again.

Marion also said that Lorendo received letters from Coach Wally Butts, head coach of the University of Georgia football team, on a regular basis. He said the letters were upbeat and always ended with encouragement; Butts said that he was looking forward to Lorendo rejoining the team after the conflict.

Gene Lorendo on LST-789 in the Pacific Theater in WWII.

CHAPTER ELEVEN:

SEEING ACTION: THE BATTLES OF IWO JIMA AND OKINAWA

A U.S. naval victory at Midway Island opened the way to U.S. control of the Mariana Islands—Guam, Saipan, and Tinian. On 18 January 1945, LST 789 departed Pearl Harbor for Eniwetok in the Marshall Islands. Next stop was Saipan and Tinian in the Marianas Islands.

On board the LST were the seven officers and 229 men of Company C, First Battalion, 14th Division, 25th Marines, plus a cargo of Marine vehicles. At Saipan, they loaded on seventeen Landing Vehicle/Vessels (LVTs), amphibious vehicles with tracks that could travel in water or on land, and 200 more Marines.

On February 12 and 13, a final dress rehearsal for Iwo Jima was held off of Tinian Island, the same island from which the B29 bomber crews would later depart with the atomic bombs that were dropped on Japan.

Iwo Jima's importance to the American military was its location almost midway between Saipan, where the American B-29 bombers were based, and Japan. Iwo Jima was 760 miles south of Japan, with three airfields and a large number of Japanese fighter planes.

The new B-29 bombers had a range of 3,500 miles, but Iwo Jima and the enemy airfields were major obstacles. Iwo Jima lay right in the flight path of the B-29s and their bombing missions to Japan. The B-29s barely had enough fuel to make the bombing run to Japan and return to their bases in the Marianas Islands. The

Japanese were also using Iwo Jima as an early warning system to relay the messages by radio that an American bomber raid was on the way to Japan.

It became obvious to the American military leaders that they must gain control of Iwo Jima if they were going to defeat Japan. The Air Force bombers had been dropping their bombs on Iwo Jima for over a month. Many of the bombers were limping back to their bases after being hit with anti-aircraft fire or having been attacked by the Japanese fighters based at Iwo Jima. The Navy, with a large flotilla of ships, had been pounding Iwo Jima for several weeks.

The 21,000 Japanese soldiers on Iwo Jima were dug-in in their network of bunkers, underground tunnels with hidden and camouflaged artillery. They were well fortified with their machine guns, mortars, land mines, and heavy artillery, and they were zeroed in on the beach where the Americans would have to land. Their defensive plan had been studied for months, addressing every detail. Iwo Jima was a heavily defended "stone fort." One Marine described Iwo Jima as an ugly place. The Japanese were ready and waiting for the Americans.

Iwo Jima is actually a small pear-shaped island two miles wide and four miles long formed by two dormant volcanoes and composed mainly of lava rock. The Japanese had built a solid stone fortress into the lava rock base with tunnels and caves and created a large fifteen-foot high terrace of ground-up volcanic ash on the beaches in anticipation of the American invasion and attack. One Marine said it was like walking or climbing on coffee grounds, making it difficult for the soldiers to climb or crawl up the terrace. Digging a foxhole was an almost impossible task. As soon as a hole was dug, it filled back up again with the ground-up volcanic ash. The Marines experienced a lot of unanticipated problems with their vehicles and tanks in attempting to scale the terraces.

After Pearl Harbor was bombed and the Japanese had taken a number of the islands in the Pacific, many in the states felt the next attack would be on the west coast of the United States. The American military wanted to strike the homeland of Japan and Iwo Jima was the first Japanese territory to be targeted by the

Americans. The top military brass knew the casualties would be costly for the invasion of Iwo Jima. They had studied their options and made the decision that they only had one choice: Attack Iwo Jima and gain control of this key island.

THE BATTLE OF IWO JIMA

As the sun came up on 19 February 1945, a large flotilla of ships, composed of more than 800 vessels, was in position. The Marine and Army assault force totaled 70,000 men. The entire invading force including the Army, Navy, and Coast Guard was more than 111,000 men. Including the crews of all the vessels, the total was more than 250,000. General "Howling Mad" Smith of the Marine Corps was the leader of the expeditionary force to attack Iwo Jima. General Smith, a graduate of Auburn (Class of 1900) and a native of Seale, Alabama, was quoted as saying, "I knew we would win the battle. But the contemplation of the cost in lives caused me many sleepless nights."

LST 789 was one of seventeen LSTs, and each one loaded with fifteen or more LVTs and all manned by Coast Guard personnel. One writer wrote, "When all the LVTs were launched, it was like all the cats in the world had kittens."

On LST 789, coxswain pilot Gene Lorendo and the other coxswains were loading their LVTs with Marines for the trip in to the southeastern shore and beach. Gene said the first wave went in with a minimum of resistance and little enemy fire. They felt the first wave had gone too smoothly—"Almost like a walk in the park on Sunday afternoon." Everyone thought it was too easy.

As soon as the first wave of Marines were on the beach and began to advance up the large terrace of ground-up volcanic ash and lava, the Japanese zeroed in on their targets and cut loose with all of their deadly firepower.

Years later, when recounting that experience, Gene told me that the second trip in was unbelievable. As he piloted his LVT toward the beach, Gene, who was the only man on the boat with his head above the vessel's armature, could see the scene they were approaching. What he saw were bodies everywhere, blood and body parts floating in the water. He had a tough time getting his vessel into position to land on the beach and lower the ramp for unloading. He felt for the young Marines who were walking into a wall of firepower from machine guns, mortars, and artillery.

Some of the LVTs were hit with enemy fire. Shells were exploding all around and there was chaos on the beach. Men were screaming, yelling, and cussing. Gene said he was "scared to death." He said he would never forget those Marines (one of whom was Jack Simms of Auburn, a talented writer and former journalism professor at Auburn University) and their young platoon leader, a second lieutenant, as he drove the LVT on to the beach and lowered the ramp.

Once his cargo of Marines had exited, Gene quickly backed off from the beach and retreated at full speed back to his LST. When all the Marines had been taken ashore, the LVTs then began loading and unloading their equipment and cargo. On D-Day plus four days, they rendezvoused with their group of LSTs and departed. The battle was won almost twenty-two days later. The Japanese lost 20,000 men with around 1,000 surrendering. The Marines lost 5,453 men with 16,134 wounded. Most of the casualties were Marines, but the battle cost America 6,821 men and 19,000 wounded.

Once the Americans had control of Iwo Jima, they quickly rebuilt the airfields. After Iwo Jima was secured, the Air Force and their B-29s based in the Mariana Islands could now commence with their bombing raids on Japan. The first raids were on March 9 and 10,1945. The damaged and wounded B-29s now had a place to land after their raids on Japan. Incidentally, one of the first B-29 crews to make an emergency landing had a side gunner by the name of Joe Connally, who would later be one of Gene Lorendo's teammates on the University of Georgia football team and then an assistant football coach with Lorendo at Auburn University.

Gilbert Seaman Hits Iwo Jima

By News-Tribune Correspondent

Coast Guardsman Gene L. Lorendo, S 1-c, box 742, Gilbert, is shown manning an anti-aircraft gun aboard the coast guard-manned tank landing ship on which he is stationed. Serving in the Pacific, Lorendo's ship landed marines and equipment on the beach of Iwo Jima. He saw plenty of action.

Lorendo at Iwo Jima in 1944.

THE BATTLE OF OKINAWA

After their time in Iwo Jima, Gene and his Coast Guard unit proceeded on to Guam in the Mariana Islands for repair of their LST 789, and then on to Leyte in the Philippines, where they loaded 460 men of the Army's 383 Regimental Combat Team for the assault on Okinawa.

The Japanese on Okinawa had to be defeated for the Americans to advance on to their final objective of Japan. There were plans to use Okinawa, a much larger island than Iwo Jima, as a base for air operations in the invasion of the Japanese mainland. Both of these islands would be staging areas for the American attack on Japan when secured.

LST 789 at Okinawa

The code name for the Okinawa invasion was "Operation Iceberg." This was the largest amphibious assault in the Pacific of WWII and was the last major battle of the war with Japan, though at the time the American forces were unaware this was to be the last major campaign. Everyone assumed the last battleground would be the invasion of Japan, another bloodbath with heavy causalities—an invasion that everyone referred to as the "Big One."

The Okinawa islands lie 385 miles southwest of Japan and northeast of Taiwan and the Philippines. They are composed of fifty or more islands, the largest being Okinawa, which is sixty miles in length and ranged from two to eighteen miles in width. LST 789 arrived at Okinawa at high tide on Easter morning, April

1, 1945, and immediately launched their LVTs loaded with Army assault forces and Marines.

For the next fifteen days, Gene and his fellow Coast Guardsmen unloaded soldiers, Marines, equipment, and all types of cargo including food, medical supplies, and ammunition. This invasion was a major military campaign with 540,000 Marines and Army personnel involved plus more than 1,600 ships—more than D-Day at Normandy.

LVT at Okinawa. Gene Lorendo was the driver or coxswain of this type of craft.

The Japanese were dug into their caves and tunnels. The terrain was a challenge for the Americans as they battled their way across the island. A surprise for the Coast Guardsmen was their 'ole basic training instructor (and former heavyweight boxing champion) Commander Jack Dempsey, who showed up to join the battle. Dempsey, who was by then in his late forties, came because he wanted to be with his men in the battle. Dempsey was later quoted as saying he "helped train thousands of men in another kind of fighting, other than boxing. These men were going into combat and their lives were at stake. There is nothing fair about war."

This battle lasted eighty-three days and over those days Okinawa was a costly battle. Some 12,500 Marines and Army troops were killed and 36,500 were wounded. The Japanese lost more than one hundred thousand men and over ten thousand were taken prisoner. This was the highest number of casualties in the Pacific Theater.

The crew of LST 789 did experience the excitement of shooting down a Japanese (Nakajima Ki-43-llb) "Oscar" fighter, but in addition to the loss of their fellow servicemen in battle, they and the whole country also experienced the loss of two great men: President Franklin Delano Roosevelt died on April 12; shortly thereafter, on April 18, Ernie Pyle, the famous war correspondent, was killed in Okinawa. Finally, on May 8, a bit of good news arrived. Germany had surrendered.

Gene Lorendo was unaware at the time that his future offensive line coach and head basketball coach at the University of Georgia, Ralph "Shug" Jordan, was also in the battle at Okinawa. Gene would later work for Shug as an assistant coach at Auburn for twenty-five years. Shug, who was a major in the Army, had seen his share of combat in the landings of North Africa, Sicily, Italy, and finally Normandy. After being wounded at Normandy, he had been sent to a hospital in England, back to the states, and then on to the Pacific and Okinawa for another battle. It should also be noted that the father of Gene Chizik, Auburn's former head football coach of the 2010 national championship team, was one of the brave Marines who fought in this famous World War II battle.

CHAPTER TWELVE:

THE "BIG ONE" AND THE SURRENDER OF JAPAN

LST 789 spent most of the month of July back in the Guam area undergoing repair and preparing for the next anticipated invasion, thought to be Japan. The "Big One."

Meanwhile, the U.S Air Force was pounding Japan with their B-29 Super Fortresses Bombers flying out of the Marianas Islands. On a May 25, 1945, bombing raid to Japan, the Americans lost 26 of the 464 planes. One of the major differences in the war with Japan and Germany was the American industrial complex and their ability to continue replacing the planes, equipment, and supplies needed to wage war.

The next development of the war in the Pacific was a shock to the crew of LST 789 and everyone else. An American B-29 bomber dropped an atomic bomb ("Little Boy," which was developed at Los Alamos, New Mexico) on Hiroshima, a military port in Japan, on August 6, 1945. A second plutonium type bomb ("Fat Man," which was developed in Hanford, Washington) was dropped on Nagasaki, another military port, on August 9. Approximately 100,000 Japanese were killed with these two atomic bombs.

The commanding admiral of the Japanese Imperial Navy reported to the Emperor of Japan, "Hell is upon us." Five days later, on August 14, 1945, and nearly four years after the attack on Pearl Harbor, the Japanese surrendered.

In preparation for the official surrender ceremony, LST 789 received orders to proceed to Tokyo Bay, Japan. The major concern for all US naval ships at this time was the minefields in Tokyo Bay. The minesweepers had done their jobs in clearing the bay of mines, but there was a fear that there were still a few isolated mines floating around in the bay. This kept everyone on edge.

They beached on the seaplane ramp at the airport of Yokosuka Naval Base. Here they delivered a unit and their equipment before anchoring at Yokosuka 300 yards from the battleship *USS Missouri*.

Gene Lorendo and the crew of LST 789 were present near the historic event on the *USS Missouri*. There were 280 American ships anchored in Tokyo Bay. (My editor's father, Lee Lamar, was also in the bay at that time on the *USS New Mexico*.) The aircraft carriers and their escorts plus hundreds of other ships remained out at sea in reserve positions because some military leaders thought the signing could be a trap by the Japanese. The American military leaders did not have all of their eggs in one basket. There had been 1,600 ships at the invasion of Okinawa. Many of those ships were out at sea on battle-ready status waiting to see where they would be deployed.

Official papers of surrender were signed on the main deck of the *Missouri* on September 2, 1945. General Douglas McArthur, the designated representative of the United States government to accept the surrender of Japan, was flanked by Admiral Chester Nimitz, commander of the Pacific Area, and Fleet Admiral William "Bull" Halsey. Two other war heroes were flown in for the surrender ceremony: Lt. General Jonathan Wainwright, commander of Allied Forces in the Philippines and a survivor of the famous Bataan Death

March, and Lt. General Arthur Percival, commander of the British Commonwealth Forces in the Philippines who had also been a prisoner of the Japanese.

In his remarks, General McArthur stated: "It is my earnest hope—indeed the hope of all mankind—that from this solemn occasion a better world shall emerge out of the blood and carnage of the past, a world founded upon faith and understanding, a world dedicated to the dignity of man and the fulfillment of his most cherished wish for freedom, tolerance, and justice."

After the papers of surrender were signed by McArthur and the Japanese representative, Foreign Minister Shigemitsu Mamoru, McArthur finished with these words: "Let us pray that peace be now restored to the world, and that God will preserve it always."

It was a cloudy overcast day at ten o'clock in the morning on the deck of the *USS Missouri*. As the surrender papers were officially signed at 10:30 a.m., the sun broke through the clouds. Then, in a powerful display of America's military strength, 2,000 planes were involved in a flyover. Any Japanese who doubted the strength of the American forces had to be overwhelmed with this display of military power.

Lorendo and the crew of LST 789 remained docked at the Yokosuka Naval Base for six more days following the ceremony and, the day after the signing of the surrender papers, Lorendo received orders for a top-secret mission. The details of the secret mission are not completely known, but two newspapers later reported that Lorendo and another Coast Guardsman received citations for bravery in carrying out this special mission.

According to Gene Lorendo's son, Mac, Gene and one of his Coast Guard shipmates were given the mission of delivering top-secret messages or orders to the other seven LSTs in their group, plus a number of the other 280 ships in

Tokyo Bay. According to Mac, his dad related that night had fallen by the time they had delivered all of the top-secret messages. It was a very dark night with a blackout in effect for all of the American ships in the harbor, plus there was no moon in sight on this particular night. As they tried to make their way back to their LST 789 in a motorized boat, they bumped into one of their own ships. This caused some anxious moments because of the fear of mines. It was not until the next morning at daybreak that they were finally able to find their way back to their own LST.

The tacticians of the War Department in Washington, D.C., had estimated that the United States would have suffered 500,000 casualties if the "Big One" had taken place and the invasion of Japan had been necessary. It was also stated that the war would have continued for at least two more years.

Everyone was relieved by the good news that the war was finally over, but for Gene, the news changed quickly to sadness. He was informed that his mother, Katherine, had passed away on September 8. There was no way Gene could return to Minnesota for the funeral service.

CHAPTER THIRTEEN:

A VISIT TO HIROSHIMA AND THE RETURN HOME

The crew members of LST 789 were excited with the announcement that Japan had officially surrendered. The next question from the crew was "When are we going home?"

For Lorendo and his fellow shipmates, the answer was in their just-received orders. They were to pick up 203 seamen and four officers for transportation to Guam.

It was just a "hop, skip, and a jump" from Japan to Guam—2,000 miles at thirteen miles per hour. LST 789 departed for Guam on September 10, 1945, arriving six days later and remaining moored there until September 27. The crew of LST 789 and the other seven LST's in their convey then departed for Agoo, Luzon, in the Philippine Islands, another 1,500 miles away, to pick up a load of Sixth Army, 731st Engineers unit of 149 men and their motorized equipment for a 1,500-mile return trip back to Kure, Japan.

Kure is a city in the Hiroshima Prefecture of Japan located fifteen or twenty miles from Hiroshima. In WWII, Kure served as a military and naval center and was the home base of the largest battleship ever built, the *Yamato*. The engineer company's assignment was to aid in the clean-up of Hiroshima.

In an interview fifty years later for a story that ran August 22, 1995, in the *Tribune Free Press* of Chisholm, Minnesota, about the anniversary of VJ Day, Lorendo shared this story. Since they were in the area, Captain Mulveay, a four-striper (same as a full colonel in the Army or Air Force) who was in command of the LST group and the entire convoy, wanted to see the damage at Hiroshima.

LORENDO

Lorendo volunteered to be the coxswain for Captain Mulveay and a team chosen to go ashore at Hiroshima. Gene piloted an LVT amphibious vehicle for the shore party of Coast Guardsmen and was one of the first Americans, in Gene's words "To step into this mess."

When the reporter asked Lorendo what his thoughts were of the scene, Gene responded, "I just hope nobody ever has to go through this again." But when he was asked if we should have dropped the atomic bombs, Gene's answer was, "You bet. We saved an awful lot of lives of soldiers on both sides. At the time it was the only thing to do."

My research for the Lorendo book brought with it a number of surprises. One was to learn that Gene played in the band in high school and was a member of the town orchestra. Another was to discover that Gene was a poet. Though I have not been able to find many of his poems, this one written by Gene before making the return journey home from Japan to the States captures both his poetic side and his emotions at the time:

I'm Coming Home
"I wish that I could write to you I'm coming home.
Cuz when that event happens, I'll never again roam,
I thought I'd like to sail and ride the seven seas,
But I'd just as soon be home, raking leaves from the trees.
I'd like to take my gal out and order a steak,
Then to sit thru an entire movie without a break.
It isn't much I am asking, I hope you'll understand,
Just let me get my feet back upon some solid land,
I'd like to take the car out, just for a little spin,
And to stop in at the "corner bar" for a shot of gin.
I'd like to shoot the "breeze" with my buddies for a while,
And to sit by the radio...and just to spin the dial.
There's not much hope in wishing, things don't work that way;
But we should be heading "stateside"...about the month of
May.
So, don't you get disgusted honey, I should be seeing you soon.
If not in May, I know damn well, I'll be seeing you in June."
(Written by Gene Lorendo from Japan in 1945.)

LORENDO

LST 789 earned two battle stars for her service during World War II before making the long 6,000-mile trip back to Pearl Harbor and then on to San Francisco. Much of the lengthy voyage home in LST 789 was made at a speed of eleven knots, or thirteen miles per hour. You have heard the saying "a slow boat from China." This was a slow boat from Japan.

As the crew of LST 789 finally approached San Francisco on Christmas Eve of 1945, they received a message from shore asking what the men of the ship would most like for their first meal back in the States. The answer was all the cold fresh milk they could drink and a large steak with all the trimmings.

The men of LST 789 were excited to be back in the good ole USA. They were safely back in their home country and were thankful to have survived the war. Some of LST 789's crew members were released from their duties in San Francisco. Lorendo and his friend, Marion Gilbert, were part of the crew who took LST 789 down the Pacific Coast and through the Panama Canal, up the Atlantic Ocean to the Gulf of Mexico, then to New Orleans and its final resting place at Lake Charles, Louisiana, on February 7, 1946.

Soon thereafter, Gene arrived back in the Twin Cities by train and caught a bus up to Gilbert. He was excited to be back home after his long journey and he received a war hero's welcome from the people of Gilbert with lot of pats on the back, "thanks for your service," and "glad to have you home."

Though Gene and his father were still grieving over the death of his mother, Katherine, the story goes that Gene asked his father if there were any good-looking single women around town. Gene's father said, "Yes. There are a couple up at the high school."

In those days, the local school board brought in several teachers each year from the Twin Cities to fill in their staff. One of those teachers was an attractive art and English teacher from Minneapolis named Jane Campbell, a graduate of the University of Minnesota. Once Gene and Jane met, it didn't take long for a romance to develop.

LORENDO

Gene had saved most of his military pay and he had a large amount of leave time accrued when he was discharged. Having a little money in his savings account allowed him time to ponder his future. He was not enthused with the prospect of going to work in the iron ore mines of the Mesabi Range. He had seen the men who spent their careers in the dark brown soil mining iron ore. He could easily have taken this route, but his goal earlier in life had been to be a coach. He decided to stick with his original goal.

CHAPTER FOURTEEN:

LORENDO RETURNS TO THE UNIVERSITY OF GEORGIA

During his time in the Coast Guard, Gene had received frequent letters of encouragement from Coach Wally Butts of Georgia. When he returned to Gilbert, he found more letters from Coach Butts and Coach Elmer Lampe stating his scholarship offer was still good and they hoped Gene would rejoin the team when practice opened in mid-August.

Lorendo also received a letter from Georgia's All-American back and team captain, Charlie Trippi, urging Gene to report to practice in top shape and informing him that the team was looking forward to the 1946 season with great expectations.

Seeing the scholarship as an opportunity to pursue his education and his dream of someday being a coach himself, Gene accepted the offer. Remembering how much difficulty he had experienced in 1942 with the heat and humidity of the South, however, Gene knew the weather down in Athens would be a problem for him, so he worked out every day trying to get into top physical condition by running and lifting weights.

At the same time, he and Jane were becoming more serious in their relationship and, as the date to leave for Georgia approached, they decided to get married. They tied the knot on August 7, 1946. The speed of the romance and the wedding announcement caused some controversy within the Campbell family. Jane's parents and grandparents were prominent families in Minneapolis and they could not believe their daughter and granddaughter had gone up to the Mesabi Range in northern Minnesota and married a man from the small mining town of Gilbert. With time, however, the

Campbell family grew to love and respect Gene Lorendo, the man
Jane chose to marry.

THE UNIVERSITY OF GEORGIA
DEPARTMENT OF ATHLETICS
ATHENS, GEORGIA

August 12, 1946

Dear Gene:

The University of Georgia football team is in the process
of playing the toughest schedule in its history.

As a personal favor I am asking every member of the team
to be responsible for their physical condition and cooperation
with the coaching staff throughout the season.

It is necessary that every player have the interest, spirit,
and will to pay the price for a successful season.

Sincerely,

Charley Trippi, Capt.

CT:d

*Letter from Charlie Trippi, Captain of the University of Georgia
football team, 1946.*

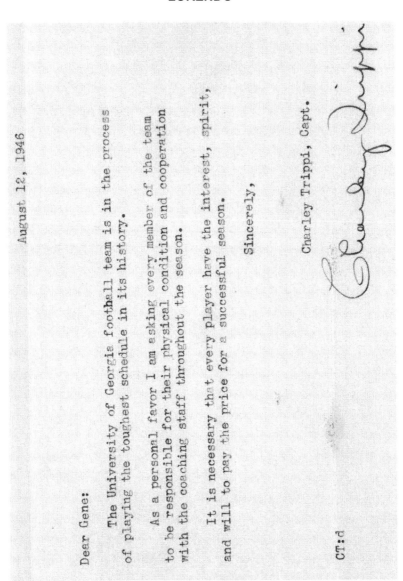

August 12, 1946

Dear Gene:

The University of Georgia football team is in the process of playing the toughest schedule in its history.

As a personal favor I am asking every member of the team to be responsible for their physical condition and cooperation with the coaching staff throughout the season.

It is necessary that every player have the interest, spirit, and will to pay the price for a successful season.

Sincerely,

Charley Trippi, Capt.

CT:d

Detail from letter from Charlie Trippi, Captain of the University of Georgia football team, 1946.

Gene and Jane Lorendo on their wedding day, August 7th, 1946.

Gene was concerned about how Coach Butts would react to the news that he was married and wondered if he had the nerve to even tell Coach Butts. It was common knowledge when Gene had first gone down to Georgia in 1942 that Butts did not like to have married players on the team. So the newlyweds decided that Gene would go down to Athens alone while Jane remained in Minnesota and continued to teach at Gilbert High School.

In mid-August 1945, Gene Lorendo said good-bye to his new bride and took the bus to the Twin Cities where he caught a train to Athens. Upon arriving at the University of Georgia, Lorendo reported to Coach Butts at the athletic complex.

Butts, who was excellent at recognizing athletic talent and saw tremendous potential in Gene Lorendo, was excited to see Gene. He remembered Gene from the summer of 1942 when he worked out with the team and then unexpectedly left to join the military before the season began. (If Gene had stayed at Georgia he would later have received a lot of flak from his Auburn friends since the 1942 Auburn Tigers, led by Monk Gafford, had upset the then-No. 1 Georgia team 27-13.)

After he arrived in Athens, Lorendo told Coach Butts, "You know I played some college football up North." Coach Butts acknowledged he was aware that Lorendo had already played some college football. He told Lorendo, "I am going to place your records in the back of the file cabinet behind the other player's records." That way, if anyone came down to inspect the team for violations, Lorendo's files might be overlooked.

When Gene had come down to Georgia in the summer of 1942 he was six-two and 185 pounds. Now in 1946, after a partial football season at Iowa State Teachers College, a season in the National Basketball League, and three years in the Coast Guard, he had filled out to six-three and 230 pounds.

In those first weeks at Georgia, Lorendo was very unhappy with his personal situation. He was too far away from Jane and, despite his efforts to prepare for it, he was suffering in the Georgia summer heat. Though he had worked out steadily before coming to Georgia, Lorendo was still not prepared for the sweltering heat and humidity of Athens in August. By the start of the season he had lost almost twenty-five pounds. He told his former Coast Guard friend Marion Gilbert, who was now a student at Mercer University in Macon,

Georgia, "The coaches have run us to death. None of my pants fit me now."

After three weeks of practice, Gene told his roommate he had decided to leave the team and return to Minnesota. His plans were to take the train to Atlanta on Saturday night, a repeat of his earlier vanishing act when Gene left the team under the cover of night in 1942. This time, though, Lorendo's roommate slipped the word to one of the assistant coaches after the team's Saturday scrimmage.

When Lorendo arrived at the train station that night, two of the assistant coaches were waiting for him. When they asked why he was leaving, Lorendo explained that he was married and he knew Coach Butts frowned on players being married. He told the coaches he had just gotten married in August and his wife, Jane, was teaching in northern Minnesota. Lorendo said the present arrangement was not going to work and he was returning to Minnesota to be with Jane.

To Lorendo's astonishment, the coaches said this was not a problem and confided in Gene that a number of the players were now married and Coach Butts had become more tolerant of married players because of the interruption in their studies by the war. Gene later learned that there were fourteen other married players on the 1946 team.

The coaches instructed Gene to go up to Minnesota, get Jane, and bring her back to Athens. They promised to get the couple an apartment and find a teaching job for Jane. It was obvious the assistant coaches had been in communication with Coach Butts, who recognized that his prize recruit was a flighty person. He remembered that Lorendo had left the team in 1942. He knew Lorendo had served in the Coast Guard during WWII in the Pacific Theatre. He also was aware that Gene's mother had died a year earlier. Then, being informed Gene had recently gotten married, Butts was aware that Lorendo had experienced a lot of emotional ups and downs in the last couple of years. But he had seen enough of Lorendo in practice to know he had tons of potential and could be an outstanding player for the Georgia Bulldogs in the future.

So Gene got on the train that night and traveled up to Minnesota, where he discussed the idea of moving to Athens with Jane. A couple of weeks later the two returned to Athens where the coaches had, indeed, gotten them an apartment and a teaching job for Jane in Athens.

One of Gene's teammates on the 1946 Georgia team said the players understood why Gene returned to Minnesota to fetch his bride once they saw Jane. He said she was a beauty: When Jane walked down the main street of Athens she turned heads.

Coach Butts kept Lorendo on the freshman/junior varsity team most of the year after he missed two weeks of fall practice going up to retrieve Jane. Still, Butts had high hopes that Lorendo would settle in and become a solid player for Georgia in the future and he took a special interest in his capricious new recruit.

Perhaps that was because Butts recognized that Lorendo, as a twenty-five-year-old married freshman, did not fit in with the other eighteen- to nineteen-year-old freshmen players. It may also have been that the two also shared something else in common: Butts' father, like Gene's, had also been a drayman in Milledgeville, Georgia.

For these and other reasons, Butts became a "Dutch uncle" to Lorendo, especially after Gene's father passed away on December 7, 1946—Gene Jr.'s twenty-fifth birthday. Gene visited with Coach Butts in his office on a regular basis, especially during football season, the two both looking forwarded to their Friday morning chats.

CHAPTER FIFTEEN:

PLAYING BETWEEN THE HEDGES: UNIVERSITY OF GEORGIA FOOTBALL

The 1946 Season

Off the football field, Wally Butts was a mild-mannered gentleman who loved animals, babies, turnip greens, and was known to be very generous. But on the football field, Butts was another man entirely. He was a tongue-lashing general who drove his players hard and demanded perfection on every play. His motto was, "You can win, if you are willing to pay the price."

Since Coach Butts was one of the most successful coaches in the nation during the 1940s, his coaching method was held in high regard by many of his peers in the coaching profession. Coach Butts was an offensive genius whose vertical passing game was considered by many to be the best in the country.

Not only did Georgia lead the SEC in passing offense thirteen of the twenty-one years with Butts at the helm, his coaching ability was so revered that he was selected for what today is the offensive coordinator for three College All-Star Football Classic games, preseason American football games that pitted the National Football League champions against a team of star college seniors from the previous year.

One sportswriter wrote in 1943 that the College All-Star team had no chance of winning the game that year, to which one of the All-Star players responded, "With Coach Butts offense, we have a chance to win."

LORENDO

Sure enough, the College All-Stars team defeated the Washington Red Skins 27-7 in 1943 and the Chicago Bears 16-0 in 1947 with Butts coaching the offense. The one game the All-Stars lost with Coach Butts in charge of the offense was to the Chicago Cardinals, who were led by one of Butts' former players, Georgia All-American and All-NFL back Charlie Trippi, in 1948.

According to Lorendo, Butts was "tough as hell," and the players at Georgia were scared to death of him. He was, after all, the dean of SEC coaches and was known as the "Little General." Butts ruled Georgia football with an iron fist and he was "Mister Georgia Football" in the forties, a time when Butts led Georgia to national prominence in college football.

Lorendo recalled that, when players were downtown in Athens and they saw Coach Butts coming down the sidewalk, they would do an about-face and double-time it in the opposite direction, duck into a store and get out of sight, or cut across the street and avoid eye contact with Butts.

One of the stories Lorendo was told about Butts during this time was that he was a fine boxer who had fought in Golden Gloves competitions in earlier years and was known to enter boxing competitions at county fairs. And he usually won the prize money. It was known that Coach Butts and one of his assistant coaches, Quinton Lumpkin, worked out by boxing a few rounds each week.

Wally Butts had played college football at Mercer University in Macon, Georgia. The story is that Mercer had hired a new coach and his name was Bernie Moore. When Coach Moore arrived at Mercer, they had a reception for the new coach. As the Mercer players greeted their new coach with "Nice to meet you," "Welcome to Mercer," etc., Wally Butts, who was a freshman, shook hands with his new coach and said, "I am your starting right end." Coach Moore was taken aback by this comment, but by the start of the season, Wally Butts was the starting right end and went on to be an All-Southern end at Mercer. (Bernie Moore would become the head coach at LSU and then go on to become the commissioner of the Southeastern Conference.)

Buck Bradberry, who later became one of Lorendo's associates on the Auburn coaching staff and who had also played for Butts at

Georgia, described Butts as a brilliant coach and a great recruiter, perhaps the best recruiter of his time.

The amazing thing about Butts was his ability to recruit outstanding players from states outside the Southeast. Among those recruits were Frank Sinkwich, an All-American and Heisman Trophy winner from Ohio; Charlie Trippi and John Rauch, both All-Americans from Pennsylvania; Zeke Bratkowski, an All-American from Illinois; Harry Babcock, an All-American from New York; and other great players, including Gene Lorendo from Minnesota.

Bradberry also noted that Coach Butts was a small man, but very tough and he expected all of his Georgia teams to be tougher than the teams the Bulldogs were playing.

When Lorendo joined the Georgia team in the fall of 1946, the twenty-five-year-old freshman was assigned to the freshman/junior varsity team, where he languished during the '46 season.

In 1946, Georgia had a very talented team led by the great All-American Charlie Trippi and including many outstanding players such as Johnny Rauch, who would later become head coach of the Oakland Raiders of the NFL, along with a squad that included All-American guard Herb St. John and players such as "Rabbit" Smith, Dick McPhee, Dan Edwards, Weyman Sellers, Joe Tereshinski, "Buck" Bradberry, and Joe Connally.

The biggest game of the season was against the Alabama Crimson Tide and the Tide's All-American back Harry Gilmer. Alabama was the defending champion of the Southeastern Conference and winner of the Rose Bowl the previous season. The game was played in Athens and Georgia's Charlie Trippi had a huge day, running for one touchdown and passing for another, as Georgia won 14 to 0. The Bulldogs continued on undefeated with a 41-0 win over Auburn and its quarterback Travis Tidwell, who was leading the nation in total offense.

The last game of the season was against Georgia Tech. Bobby Dodd's Yellow Jackets were eight and one for the year, having only lost to Orange Bowl-bound Tennessee by a score of 13 to 9. Leading the Yellow Jackets was Frank Broyles (later the head coach and athletic director at Arkansas). The Bulldogs prevailed in this rivalry game, winning 35 to 7.

A Classic College Football Series

With the win over Tech, the Bulldogs were quickly invited to the Sugar Bowl, where they were to play Carl Snavely's North Carolina Tar Heels, the champions of the Southern Conference. The Tar Heels were led by the great All-American back Charlie "Choo-Choo" Justice.

As Georgia prepared for this big ballgame, one of the questions Coach Wally Butts was asked in a pre-bowl game news conference was if his "Super Frosh," (super freshman) Gene Lorendo, would play in the bowl game? Though Lorendo had spent the season on the freshman team, he'd had a stellar year and Butts sometimes referred to Gene as his "Super Frosh."

This Georgia JV team was unbeaten in fall 1946, tying Alabama and beating Auburn twice. Their first Auburn game was in West Point, Georgia, with the Bulldogs winning 26 to 13, and during which Lorendo caught seven passes. The second game was played in Orlando, Florida, with the Bulldogs winning big again. The records do not show how many passes the "Super Frosh" caught in the second game, but it is safe to say Gene Lorendo holds the record for passes caught in any Georgia versus Auburn freshman season.

When asked this question prior to the Sugar Bowl, Butts replied, "Lorendo would travel with the team and would play in New Orleans."

The Sugar Bowl has a history of great games, but it had never encountered two groups of such rowdy partisans as Georgia and North Carolina. New Orleans was flooded by the loyal fans of these two undefeated teams. Seventy-three thousand fans crammed in to Tulane Stadium. An estimated 30,000 fans showed up without tickets, and scalpers were out in force and having a field day. World War II was over and everyone was ready to party and celebrate, so the French Quarter was jumping with students and alumni, and bookies were taking bets left and right. New Orleans was alive.

As game day—January 1, 1947—arrived, a trombone player was strutting his stuff in the North Carolina band. His name was Andy Griffith, who went on to fame on Broadway and in television and Hollywood and, later, wrote the best-selling monologue called "What It Was, Was Football."

Who had the better player, Trippi of Georgia or Justice of North Carolina? Choo Choo came into the Sugar Bowl with an average of 7.2 yards every time he carried the ball. Trippi was just a little behind at 6.5 yards per carry.

Georgia, with a fifteen-game winning streak, was favored by six points. No one seemed to notice that Art Weiner, an All-American end and outstanding receiver, had left the North Carolina team at the end of the regular season. North Carolina drew first blood with an interception, which led to a touchdown and a 7-0 halftime lead.

In the second half, Carolina had mounted a good drive when the biggest play of the game took place. Walt Pupa, the NC quarterback, dropped back to pass when Joe Tereshinski, Georgia's defensive end, leaped high to intercept the pass at the Georgia 32-yard line. A couple of Tar Heels grabbed Joe, but before they could get him down, he lateraled the ball to Dick McPhee, a Georgia linebacker. McPhee took off down the field with several Carolina players in hot pursue. Two of the Tar Heels finally pulled McPhee down at the 13-yard line.

This was the most controversial play in the history of the Sugar Bowl. Coach Carl Snavely of North Carolina said the lateral was a forward lateral, which is illegal. Georgia and its Coach Wally Butts stated the lateral was backwards, which would be a legal play. The game was held up for twenty minutes before the officials could restore play. No penalty was called. Georgia retained the ball and went on to score.

(Dick McPhee was later the head football coach at my high school, Rome High School in Rome, Georgia.)

Georgia won the game 20 to 10 and finished the season undefeated. Charlie Trippi was named All-American and winner of the Maxwell Award, which is given to the best college player in America. Notre Dame would go on to win the national championship, finishing with eight wins and one tie. Army, with their touchdown twins and All-Americans Doc Blanchard and Glenn Davis, finished No. 2 with a tie. The Bulldogs came in at No. 3. The Georgia fans thought the Associated Press poll had been tainted by the "powerful Midwestern" vote.

Lorendo did play in the game. His roommate on the trip was Joe Connally, another end and friend from Cairo, Georgia. Joe, who later served on Ralph "Shug" Jordan's coaching staff with Lorendo for twenty-five years, commented that Lorendo didn't always make the bed check during the Sugar Bowl in New Orleans.

Ten months later, in September of 1947, the Georgia Bulldogs traveled to Kenan Stadium in Chapel Hill, North Carolina, to continue the rivalry with the North Carolina Tar Heels and Charlie "Choo-Choo" Justice. Carolina was favored in this game since Georgia's great player Charlie Trippi was now in the NFL. With 43,000 fans looking on, Choo-Choo was the difference as North Carolina won a close game 14 to 7.

The series continued in 1948 with North Carolina traveling to Athens. The Tar Heels came into this game ranked No. 3 in the nation after a 34-0 thrashing of the Texas Longhorns. Georgia was led by their All-American quarterback Johnny Rauch and an outstanding end corps led by Gene Lorendo and Bobby Walston.

Charlie Justice put on a show that many old-time Georgia fans say was one of the greatest performances ever in Sanford Stadium. Choo-Choo was involved in all three touchdowns. A Rauch-to-Lorendo touchdown pass made it close in the fourth quarter, but the day belonged to Justice. North Carolina won 21-14. Justice, a two-time runner-up for the Heisman Trophy, was beaten out for the award that year by Leon Hart of Notre Dame, but a lot of sportswriters felt the Midwestern vote had been a factor in the selection process and Justice should have received the Heisman award.

Another big game that year that Lorendo recalled in our interviews was the LSU game played in Tiger Stadium. The game was scoreless in the first half and the Bulldogs had played horribly. When the team entered the dressing room at halftime, Coach Butts kicked one of the team trunks and injured his foot. With the team doctor and trainer addressing the injured Butts, assistant coach J.B. "Ears" Whitworth climbed up on a table. Lorendo recalled Coach Whitworth saying, "You players are killing Coach Butts with your play."

"Assistant coach Quinton Lumpkin climbed up on the table and chewed our asses up one side and down the other," said Lorendo. According to Lorendo, the double doors to the dressing room opened inward, but after the tongue-lashing by Coach Lumpkin, the players were all riled up and ready to play. They were like a wild herd of buffalo. When the word came for the team to run back on to the field, they simply knocked the doors off the hinges.

Georgia dominated the LSU Tigers for the remainder of the game, winning 22-0. After the game Coach Butts told the team they played like real Dogs in the second half. He then added, "Don't worry about those dammed doors, I will take care of that situation."

From there, the Bulldogs went on to play against their in-state rivals, Georgia Tech, a game recounted in detail by Ralph McGill, then the sports editor of the *Atlanta Constitution*. His play-by-play summary of the game captures it all perfectly:

Georgia vs Georgia Tech 1948
By Ralph McGill, Sports Editor, **Atlanta Constitution**
Sanford Stadium, Athens, Georgia

For seven minutes nothing had happened. The teams of Georgia Tech and Georgia had fought up and down the field, both hitting hard and each taking blows well.

Then John Rauch dropped back crouching and searching the field as his receivers broke down field. His blockers were fending off the furious rush of the Techs. But there was not much time. Down field and to his right, he saw Gene Lorendo break quickly into the open.

LORENDO

Rauch threw, the ball, wet from the soggy field, was for a moment black in the sky, and then Lorendo leaped up with two Tech men. Six hands reached for the ball. Lorendo's two hands got it. Lorendo whirled and broke away from grasping arms. He suddenly was running in the open. Tech tacklers were flung aside with a stiff arm. He went storming along like a maddened giant to the Tech 32. He had cracked the Tech defense. He had shaken it up, he had hurt Tech as a heavyweight fighter hurts an opponent with a hard right to the jaw. Before it could find itself again, the swift Georgia backs had driven on to score. It was the first of three touchdowns that defeated Tech 21-13 and brought a Conference Championship to Athens. The game turned on Lorendo's great catch and on his thundering run which broke the hearts of the defenders. Before the Tech defense could again organize itself, Joe Geri, the Pennsylvania Phantom, and Rauch's passes to Lorendo, the Georgia machine had driven 93 yards to a second touchdown.

You would not want a finer boy to have done it. Gene Lorendo from Gilbert, Minnesota, served in combat with the Coast Guard in the Pacific. He was cited twice for heroism and came back laden with medals attesting to his combat spirit and courage.

Yesterday, in a friendly game, but still a combat test, it was he who broke, temporarily, the Tech defense. After the first two touchdowns through the breach made by the Minnesotan, Georgia could not score through the tech defense. Only when Lorendo had shaken the defense could the Bulldogs score through it.

There followed a pass from Rauch to Lorendo, the right end for Georgia. Lorendo ran like a corn-fed bull from his native state of Minnesota, literally tearing himself out of the clutches of two tacklers and stiff-arming another out of the way for a total of 38 yards. Georgia's tremendously powerful line play, the passing of John Rauch, the running of Joe Geri, and the pass catching of Gene Lorendo all contributed to the Georgia victory.

The eighth-ranked Dogs received a bid to play Texas in the Orange Bowl. The Longhorns were led by a big running back, Tom Landry, later to become the famous coach of the Dallas Cowboys. This game was a real offensive duel. With Texas leading late in the game 34-28, Georgia made a last-ditch effort to score and win the game, but fell short. Texas got the ball back and scored another touchdown to win 41-28. Landry had been the difference in this big ballgame and was named MVP.

Gene's Final Football Year at Georgia

Joe Connally, Gene's teammate and another end, related that Coach Butts made the decision in 1949 season to play Lorendo mostly on offense since he was Georgia's best pass receiver. Butts' offense called for Lorendo to run longer and deeper pass routes down field. Connally and Lorendo were buddies who enjoyed trying to get under the other's skin. Joe would be the starter at defensive end. When Georgia was kicking off, Joe would say to Lorendo, "Looks like I am starting today." Lorendo was not happy with this comment. Lorendo would still play a lot of the game on defense. Lorendo felt he was the starter at end.

The rivalry series with North Carolina and their senior All-American Charlie Justice continued in 1949 with the Tar Heels prevailing again 21-14. As the Georgia team was leaving the field in Chapel Hill, a North Carolina assistant coach ran over to Coach Butts and said this player Lorendo looked like the same player who played against him up at the Iowa State Teachers College in Waterloo, Iowa, in 1942. Coach Butts said it must have been another Lorendo. Of course it was the one and only Gene Lorendo.

In 1949 Coach Pat Dye saw his first college football game in Athens. Georgia was playing Alabama and the Tide won a hard-fought football game 14-7. What did Pat remember about that game? "Seeing Gene Lorendo hit an Alabama running back, knocking his helmet off, and the helmet rolling ten yards down the field. Lorendo was tough."

Gene Lorendo, University of Georgia Football, 1949.

LORENDO

The Georgia Bulldogs and Coach Wallace Butts had nine consecutive winning seasons from 1939 through 1948. With their All-American quarterback, Johnny Rauch, having graduated, Georgia struggled in 1949, losing four of their games by less than a touchdown. In Lorendo's senior season, the Dogs lost six games, won four, and tied one.

Despite the disappointing outcome of the 1949 season, Gene Lorendo still had a great year, leading the Southeastern Conference in pass receiving in '49. During his years at Georgia, Gene more than made up for missing out on playing in the Rose Bowl back in 1942 by playing in three consecutive bowl games—the Sugar, Gator, and Orange bowls—before he graduated from the University of Georgia with a bachelor's degree in education.

And, while Lorendo excelled at football and became a star player on the gridiron, he also had the opportunity to play—and play well—his favorite sport on the boards, basketball.

CHAPTER SIXTEEN:

COURT TIME: UNIVERSITY OF GEORGIA BASKETBALL

If you asked any college basketball player of Gene Lorendo's era to tell you what their goals or dreams were, most would answer that they wanted the opportunity to play in the NCAA tournament and the final four.

If you dug a little deeper on their bucket list, though, many players would indicate their desire to play in New York City's Madison Square Garden, "The World's Most Famous Arena." Gene Lorendo, a freshman forward, and his new coach, Ralph "Shug" Jordan, of the University of Georgia basketball team had that opportunity on December 6, 1946.

Jordan had come to Georgia the same year as Lorendo, replacing Elmer Lampe who had been the primary coach recruiting Gene Lorendo to Georgia. Not long after Gene arrived on the University of Georgia campus and just before the start of fall college football season in 1946, Lampe resigned from his position as Georgia's head basketball coach and assistant football coach to accept a position at Dartmouth, an Ivy League college in New Hampshire. The coach who replaced Lampe at Georgia was Shug Jordan, for whom Gene would later serve as an assistant coach at Auburn.

The Bulldogs were scheduled to play their opening game of the season against St. John's University, the No. 2-ranked college basketball team in the nation, at Madison Square Garden.

The Georgia team arrived in New York by train the afternoon of December 4. When they arrived at their hotel, the seventeen-story high Belvedere a couple of blocks from Times Square and

Broadway, one of the players who had never stayed in a hotel higher than three or four stories asked Coach Jordan what the players should do if an emergency should take place on one of the upper floors. Shug answered, "The coaches and first team players will take the elevator and the other players should take the steps or the fire escape." The fire escapes were on the outside of the building.

That night the Georgia team watched a National Basketball Association (NBA) game between the New York Knickerbockers and the Detroit Falcons at Madison Square Garden. Two days later, they took to the Garden's court themselves to play St. John's before 18,000 fans.

St. John's Coach Joe Lapchick's talented team was led by two All-Americans: point guard and super playmaker Dick ("Dickie") McGuire and six-foot nine-inch center Harry Boykott. St. John's is one of the most heralded college basketball programs in the country, with twenty-seven appearances in the NCAA tournament and ranked in the top five teams to play in the NCAA championship along with Kentucky, Kansas, North Carolina, and Duke. (Surprisingly, the list does not include UCLA.)

During the game, Lorendo hit a couple of long one-handed push shots early in the contest to keep Georgia in the running, but the St. John's Redmen, directed by the smooth and efficient Dickie McGuire, slowly took control of the game. With a big lead in the second half, Coach Lapchick went to his bench and substituted freely. Then, as Georgia started to cut into the lead, he sent his starting five back in to finish the game. St. John's won the game with a score of 66-43.

After the game Coach Lapchick apologized to Coach Jordan for putting his starting five back in the game. Lapchick explained to Jordan, "It was the spread." Coach Jordan didn't know what Coach Lapchick was talking about. "Spread?" Coach Lapchick explained, "The point spread."

Lorendo finished the game having scored ten points, with most of those points coming from his "downtown" (long) shots. Al Fabian and Bob Healy added eleven and nine points for Georgia. McGuire had ten points and guard Len Doctor scored eighteen for the St. John's team.

Gene had made five long field goals in the game, a record that matched an equal number of field goals by Gene's hoop hero, All-American Hank Luisetti of Stanford, when he played in Madison Square Garden during the 1939 season. Though Luisetti, who was Player of Year in college basketball for the 1939-40 season, was one of the greatest players of all time and had been a media sensation of the "Big Apple" in 1939, few people seemed to notice that Lorendo had also hit five field goals from long range in 1946.

Dick McGuire went on to be a seven-time NBA All-Star, a member of the Naismith College Hall of Fame, and a coach in the NBA. (His brother Al, played at St. John's from 1947 to 1951 and then coached Marquette University to an NCAA national championship in 1977 before going on to be a color commentator for NBC and college basketball for several seasons.)

Following the weekend in the Big Apple, the team traveled to Buffalo, New York, to play in a holiday tournament. Georgia played Niagara University in the first game of a double bill. The second game was Canisius vs. Oklahoma A&M (now Oklahoma State). The new coach at Canisius, Earl Brown, was very optimistic about the upcoming season. He was a Notre Dame graduate who would soon become the head football coach at Auburn (1948-1950), only to be replaced by Shug Jordan in 1951.

In January 1947, Georgia met Alabama in a big SEC basketball game in Athens, Georgia. Alabama came into the game with a nine-game winning streak and was led by "Big Jim" Homer at center.

Dick McKensie, a starting guard and captain of the Alabama team from Selma, Alabama, (Dick and his wife, Rosemary, were good friends of ours from "Food for the Soul" Sunday School Class at Auburn United Methodist Church) recalled a point in the game when one of his teammates, a young Alabama forward, came over to the Bama bench during a timeout and announced to the team, "I am going to get this big guy Lorendo."

Dick recalled reaching across the team huddle, grabbing the young forward by his jersey, and saying, "This guy Lorendo loves to fight. He will take on our whole team. Don't you dare start anything."

Lorendo had eighteen points in that game and led Georgia with ten rebounds; however, Alabama and Big Jim pulled the game out in the last few minutes.

Gene's reputation as a fighter was well earned. Coach Jordan used to enjoy telling the story of a pure shooting forward he had recruited while Lorendo was playing at Georgia. The forward was very smooth, with a deft technique he had developed to perfection in which he would push the defensive player off with his left forearm, receive the pass from the guard, send his pure shot on the way to the goal, and...swish!

Shug often matched Lorendo up with this forward in practice and, when the shooter scored, Shug would chew Lorendo out for letting him score without a hand in his face. When Gene complained about the shooter pushing him off, Shug would say, "Gene you have to guard your man and get a hand in his face."

Finally, Lorendo had had all he could take of this situation and at practice the next day, Gene told the shooter, "If you push me off with a forearm, I'm going to let you have it." Sure enough, the shooter came down the court and pushed Lorendo off with his forearm. Lorendo responded with a big right forearm. Bam, the shooter went down like he was shot. The next day the shooter didn't show up for practice. He was gone. Shug said, "Lorendo ran off the best player on the team."

The Tennessee Rivalry

In one of the early games of Gene's basketball career at Georgia, the Bulldogs played host to the Tennessee Volunteers in Athens and the two teams began what would be a volatile rivalry. There was something about Tennessee that caused Georgia's blood to boil whenever they tangled with the Vols.

Sonny Dragoin, former All-American wrestler and NCAA Hall of Fame golf coach at Auburn, recalled a story from that time that was passed on to him by a friend who was an assistant basketball coach at Tennessee when this game was played.

Early in the game, Lorendo was driving toward the goal for an apparent layup. A young, talented Tennessee forward slammed into Gene with a hard foul trying to prevent him from making the easy layup. Lorendo calmly stepped to the foul line and hit both foul shots. As Gene and the young Tennessee forward ran down to the other end of the court, Lorendo moved up close to the player and said, "The next time you get the ball I am going to put your ass up in the grandstand." The young forward didn't score for the remainder of the game. According to the assistant coach, the player was scared to death.

Georgia traveled to Knoxville the next season for their next encounter with Tennessee. The Vols came away with another victory, but the Georgia players and Coach Jordan were very upset with the officiating in the contest. Georgia felt one of the officials let Tennessee get away with murder in this ballgame. There was a lot of shoving and pushing under the basket and, whenever Georgia retaliated, they usually ended up with a foul being called on the Bulldogs. Things almost got out of control on a number of occasions.

In a later game the same year, the two teams met in the SEC basketball tournament. The Georgia players and coaches were furious when they saw that the same official who had called the game in Knoxville was officiating this game.

Everyone thought a brawl could develop any minute, and near the end of the heated contest, Lorendo and the big Tennessee center were on the floor fighting for a loose ball. Lorendo had gained clear possession of the ball when this same official jumped in late and called a jump ball. In his frustration with the call, Lorendo shoved the Tennessee player down with a forearm and busted his lip. The official called a technical foul on Lorendo and threw him out of the game. The Georgia fans reacted by throwing items, including a bottle, onto the court. The Tennessee player had to leave the game and did not return. This game was not a tea party. This was a war. Georgia lost the game to Tennessee 58-45, but

Georgia went down fighting and Lorendo led Georgia with fourteen points and ten rebounds.

Gene Lorendo, University of Georgia Basketball, 1948.

The Point Shaving Scandal

One of the biggest games of the year for the Georgia Bulldogs in the 1948-49 basketball season was with the defending national champions, the Kentucky Wildcats. Coach Jordan's Georgia team, which was hosting the game in Woodruff Hall in Athens, Georgia, was facing a Kentucky team with a record of sixteen wins and one loss.

Kentucky's starting five for that season were called the "Fabulous Five" by sportswriters, and they and the Wildcat team were led by All-Americans Ralph Beard and Alex Goza. Beard was a speedy five-foot ten-inch guard who was quick as a cat, a sharpshooter, and a tenacious defensive player. Goza was a talented six-seven center who could score inside or outside. Every player on the Kentucky team, coached by the legendary Adolph Rupp, was an All-American in high school.

The Dogs were in the game for only a few minutes before Kentucky raced away with their fast-break offense and sharp outside shooting. The final score was Kentucky 84 and Georgia 45. Ralph Beard had nineteen points, with a lot of his points coming on the fast break, and Alex Goza had ten. For the Bulldogs, Bob Healy had fifteen points, while his Georgia teammate, Lorendo, had ten points and ten rebounds.

Kentucky went on to win the national championship for the 1949 season, but this game and the entire season came under close scrutiny when three of the Kentucky players, including Beard and Goza, were indicted in a point shaving scandal.

This was the biggest story in college basketball in 1951. Seven colleges and thirty-three players were caught up in this plot by gamblers to purposely hold down the score in college basketball games. Three of the colleges were in New York City, including City College of New York (CCNY), a perennial basketball power, which basically received the "death penalty," the NCAA's harshest penalty that bans a school from competing in a sport for at least one year. After that, CCNY de-emphasized basketball and became a Division III program. Kentucky was put on probation and not allowed to play college basketball for the 1952-53 season.

Though this betting scandal was not the death of college basketball, it did cause the NCAA to discontinue playing the championship game in Madison Square Garden.

In response to the news of the ruling, Lorendo, who was known for his one-liners, said, "If Kentucky was shaving points against our Georgia team, beating us by thirty-nine points, I sure as hell would hate to play them when they were not shaving points."

The Georgia basketball team. Lorendo is on the left back row. Shug Jordan is on the right.

Back to the Court, for a While

After a big football victory over their rival Georgia Tech on November 27, 1948, Georgia and Georgia Tech tipped off their basketball season the next week in the ole Tech Gym in Atlanta. The game was a sell-out and a "tail" was crammed into every available seat.

LORENDO

John Bradberry, a sportswriter for the *Atlanta Constitution*, wrote in his column of the game: "About the middle of the first half, the Georgia coach puts in a man named Lorendo, and the Tech fans let out one of the most beautiful Bronx cheers (a "boooooo") you have ever heard. It seems that this man Lorendo is not a popular figure in Tech circles, which is understandable because he also plays end for Wallace Butts' football team and the picture of him catching those passes and refusing to be tackled on Sanford Field on November 27, is still fresh in the memory."

As Lorendo approached his senior year in August of 1949, just before football practice had begun at Georgia, he stopped by Coach Butts' office for a friendly chat. Coach Butts was in a jovial mood. He and Gene were having a cordial conversation when Lorendo dropped a bomb on Coach Butts: "Some of my teammates on the basketball team feel that I could be an outstanding player this coming season if I just concentrated on basketball."

Lorendo was careful not to mention his basketball coach, Shug Jordan, who was the offensive line coach for the football team. Perhaps Lorendo was also careful because Shug had become not just a coach to Gene, but also a friend, a relationship that developed on the many road trips they took to games.

When the Georgia basketball team played on the road, they traveled in a three-car caravan. Jordan, who had a big black Buick sedan, was the lead car and he always took the three largest players on the Georgia team in his car, including Gene Lorendo and Bob Healy, who always rode with Coach Jordan. An assistant coach drove the second car with four more players and a manager drove the third car with another four players.

According to Lorendo, they knew where all of the good hamburger or barbeque joints were along their route and, during those long road trips to Lexington, Nashville, Knoxville, and other SEC campuses, he and Jordan became close.

Despite Lorendo's effort to carefully broach the idea of him leaving the football team, Coach Butts did not take it sitting down. In fact, said Lorendo, Butts stood up—all five feet six inches of him—from his chair and his face turned a cherry red, the veins on his face and neck popped out, and he replied, "You Eskimo SOB, I brought you down here to play football and don't you ever forget it. I don't want to hear another damn word about basketball."

Interestingly, Lorendo did not play basketball his senior year at Georgia even though he was one of the top returning players on the Georgia team from the 1948-49 season. A little clarity came to this situation after Gene graduated from Georgia in the summer of 1950 and was hired as assistant football coach and head basketball coach at Presbyterian College in South Carolina. When Walter Johnson, Presbyterian's athletic director, announced the hiring of Lorendo, one of the reasons given for picking Lorendo was his recent success in coaching the Georgia freshman basketball team to a 9-2 winning season.

CHAPTER SEVENTEEN:

LORENDO'S FIRST COACHING JOB AT PRESBYTERIAN COLLEGE

Gene Lorendo, a versatile athlete, had lettered in three sports at the University of Georgia, was an outstanding pass-catching end on the football team, and led the SEC in receiving in 1949. He had played three years of basketball for the Bulldogs and Coach "Shug" Jordan and had run the hurdles on the track team for Coach "Spec" Towns.

After completing his senior season in football in the fall of 1949, he was expected to play another year on the Bulldog's basketball team, for which he had been a starter at forward and one of the top scorers on the team in the 1948-49 season. But Gene, who had already taken a number of detours and turns in his first twenty-nine years of life, took yet another by not returning to the basketball team for the 1949-50 season.

The reason for this had a lot to do with his family life, or rather his family finances.

By this time he and his wife, Jane, already had one son, Cam, who was born in 1949, and Jane was pregnant with another son, McLean, who was born May 9, 1951. Though Jane had taught school in Athens since they arrived there in 1946, with Cam to care for and Mac on the way, she was unable to work. Like so many married college students and athletes of today, the Lorendos were having financial problems.

Though Gene had been drafted by the Green Bay Packers of the NFL, taking that option was not an ideal solution to their financial woes. The average pay for an NFL rookie was $5,000 a season, but there were no guaranteed contracts, and even if he made the team, the contract would only be for one year. If he didn't make the team, he would be without a job and have no income to support his wife and two children.

Coach Wally Butts, who was the athletic director as well as head coach football coach at the University of Georgia, and Jordan, who was head basketball coach, helped Lorendo find a solution as he finished his senior year of college. They gave him a part-time job as coach for the Georgia men's freshman basketball team, a team Gene coached to a nine to two record and an experience that would pay a big dividend for Lorendo after he graduated.

Gene had made the decision to pursue a career in coaching after graduating from high school back in Minnesota in 1939. Now, as he was about to receive his diploma and graduate from the University of Georgia, he was faced with the task of finding a full-time coaching job, and such jobs were scarce. So he put out the word to Coach Butts and others that he was seeking a coaching job and they got busy helping him find one.

Coach Butts was close friends with Walter Johnson, who had been a successful head football coach at Presbyterian College (PC) in Clinton, South Carolina, and had been promoted to athletic director in 1946. Butts contacted Johnson on behalf of Gene and soon found out that Johnson was, indeed, looking for an assistant coach for the Presbyterian Blue Hose football team.

This was a great opportunity for any coach looking to enter the coaching profession, but then Walter Johnson added a second requirement for this position—that this person would also be the head basketball coach. It was a perfect fit for Lorendo and Coach Butts gave Gene a strong recommendation for both jobs. Soon after, Gene was hired to coach for the Blue Hose.

Gene went to work for Lonnie McMillian, the head football coach at Presbyterian and one of the sharpest football strategists in the nation. McMillian had introduced the T-formation in the South and the T-formation was the "in" offense in college football during this period of time. Armed with this innovative offense, which was used by only a few teams, McMillian's teams compiled an enviable record dotted with upsets.

LORENDO

In a somewhat ironic twist, Lorendo was hired at Presbyterian at the same time as Harry "Sid" Varney, a former football rival of Gene's, to coach the Blue Hose baseball team. Varney, a native of Pennsylvania, had starred in both football and baseball at the University of North Carolina where he was an All-American catcher in baseball and a starting guard on the football team for four years, playing in two Sugar Bowls for Coach Carl Snavely. Varney was one of the linemen clearing the way for Charlie "Choo Choo" Justice, probably the greatest offensive player to ever play at North Carolina and one of most talented backs ever to play college football, so Varney and Lorendo had squared off against each other in four Georgia/North Carolina football games, with North Carolina winning three of four. Lorendo and Varney arrived in August of 1950 just before fall practice.

Recruiting had not been strongly emphasized the previous year since there were only three coaches on the staff and two of them had just been hired. The staff worked their players hard in practice with the goal of developing them to their full potential. The staff was coaching their players up for the tough season that lay ahead.

PC's football team opened the season with Furman, a larger and much stronger team, but the Blue Hose rose to the challenge, nipping Furman 13-12. The next week, however, they were clobbered by Clemson 55-0, followed by a 21 to 6 win over Western Carolina. They went on to finish the season with five wins and five losses, ending the season with a 20-6 win over Newberry.

As soon as football season was over, Lorendo put on his second hat as basketball coach. He and Varney were both looking forward to the next season and the chance to recruit some talented players, though thanks to a PC alumnus Lorendo already had a talented squad.

Immediately following World War II, Presbyterian athletic teams were performing at a high level except for the men's basketball program, but a letter from Shag Copeland (PC Class of 1932) of Plymouth, Indiana, helped change that and had a major impact on the 1950-51 team.

LORENDO

Copeland wrote to his former coach, Lonnie McMillian, who was now head football coach, informing him of two Indiana players with special abilities and encouraging him to recruit the boys. The Presbyterian coaches recruited most of their players from North and South Carolina and Georgia, and southern Indiana was a long long way from Clinton, South Carolina. But with encouragement and insistence from Copeland, coaches McMillian and Ben Moye made the decision to travel to Indiana in the summer of 1948 in a 1936 Chevy. With Copeland as their host, they contacted and offered scholarships to Len Hawkins and Kenneth Horn.

As the coaches were preparing to return to Clinton, they asked Hawkins and Horn if they knew of any other local talent, and the two new recruits immediately told the coaches of two other players in Akron, Indiana. So on to Akron they traveled, two more hours from Clinton. There they located the local high school coach who rounded up the two players, Kay Hill and Dwight Groniger, and the PC coaches offered scholarships to them both. As they made the long drive back to Presbyterian, both coaches agreed they would most likely never see the four players again. It was a long way from Indiana to South Carolina.

A few days before school was scheduled to start in the fall, however, Coach McMillian was at football practice when an old Dodge sedan with a rack full of luggage drove on to the campus. To the coaches' surprise, all four players spilled from the car. The following 1949-50 season, two more Indiana Hoosiers joined the other four players at PC. Despite this pool of talent, however, the team was plagued with injuries that season and the team finished the season with fourteen wins and fifteen losses.

Another solid player was recruited the next season from Paducah, Kentucky—Roy Skinner, a sharp-shooting guard. (Skinner would later become the most successful coach in Vanderbilt University history, winning the SEC championship in 1965 with Clyde Lee and in 1974 with Jan Van Bredakolff. Skinner's record against Kentucky was twelve wins and sixteen losses. At some schools, a 12-16 record against your major rival will get you fired. That record against Kentucky will get you a nice raise.)

LORENDO

When Gene Lorendo arrived at PC, he was excited with the degree of talent on the Blue Hose basketball team, and even though he had only one player who was more than six feet in height, it didn't take long for the small Presbyterian College team to draw the interest of the students, alumni, and Clinton homefolks.

This "run and gun" team with a number of good shooters is still referred to as one of the greatest basketball teams in Presbyterian history, winning seventeen games and losing nine. The team broke the 100-point mark two times during the season, finishing the season with a 103-60 win over Newberry and a 102-100 win over Wofford. The team averaged 81.7 points a game, was third in the nation in scoring, set six new state records, shot seventy-seven percent from the foul line, and won their league championship. (This was way before the time of the three-point shot.)

Things were certainly going well for Gene at Presbyterian and he and Jane were happy to be in Clinton, South Carolina. The Presbyterian campus was beautiful with its giant oaks trees, azaleas, dogwoods, and shaded sidewalks. The Clinton town folks and the Presbyterian College staff had made Jane and Gene welcome at the college.

But one Saturday morning in early March 1951, Gene returned home to find out from Jane that his former Georgia coach, Shug Jordan, had called. Gene immediately phoned Jordan back and was surprised to learn that Shug was the new coach at Auburn. He had called to offer Gene an assistant coaching position on his staff coaching Auburn's receivers and offensive ends.

Lorendo would also have an additional job assignment. He would be the resident manager of Graves Center, a housing complex of cabins where all the scholarship athletes lived. The Lorendo family would live in a cabin in Graves Center, where Gene would be tasked with keeping its residents—the football and basketball players—under control and out of trouble. Gene's annual salary would be $5,000 and he would receive free housing and meals at the Graves Center cafeteria.

LORENDO

Associated Press Release, Clinton, S.C., March 22, 1951

Presbyterian College assistant coach Gene Lorendo has accepted a position as an assistant coach at Auburn, Athletic Director Walter Johnson announced today. Lorendo leaves Sunday to start spring training in his new job.

Lorendo served as both assistant football coach and as head basketball coach at PC. The former University of Georgia star led the PC Blue Hose basketball team to the Little Four and the league championship in his first year as head coach.

In announcing his decision to move to Auburn, Lorendo praised Presbyterian College, the athletic department, and Johnson. "I have thoroughly enjoyed working at Presbyterian and hate to leave," he said. "However, this is an opportunity I cannot afford to turn down. In my opinion, PC has an ideal athletic plant, one of the best in the South, regardless of the size of the school. Both the athletic department and the college administration have given me their full cooperation."

Walter Johnson also lavished high praise on his departing coach. "Lorendo did an outstanding job here and coached the best basketball team ever at PC. His football work was superlative, as evidenced by the all-around play of PC ends this fall. We'll miss him and our best wishes go with him for success in his new job."

So the Lorendos loaded up their two boys and made the move to Auburn, a place that would be home their home for another three decades.

It is interesting to note that Norm Sloan replaced Gene as head basketball coach at PC, coaching there from 1951 through 1955. Sloan would later win a national championship at North Carolina State in 1974 with the talented David Thompson, winning thirty games and losing only one. Sloan would also serve as head coach of the Florida Gators at two different times. It should also be noted that another great football coach followed Lorendo at Presbyterian. In 1954, Glenn Edward "Bo" Schembechler, the winningest coach in Michigan football history, was named PC's assistant football coach, a position he held for one year before becoming freshman coach at Bowling Green State University.

Lorendo in sweats at Presbyterian College.

CHAPTER EIGHTEEN:

"NO ONE CAN WIN AT AUBURN"

Gene Lorendo was excited to join Coach "Shug" Jordan's efforts to remedy a tough situation at Alabama Polytechnic Institute (now Auburn University). The 1950 team had lost all ten games, and the Auburn faithful were impatient.

Earl Brown, a Notre Dame graduate, was Auburn's head coach in 1950 when the Tigers did not win a game. He maintained that he should continue in his position as head coach since a year remained on his contract. Auburn fans had seen enough of Coach Brown and his three-season record of three wins, four ties, and twenty-two losses, and they wanted a change. Brown defended his tenure by claiming, "No one can win at Auburn."

Fans couldn't accept that. A group of alumni took the case to Auburn President Ralph Draughon, who opposed a change in the program, dismal though it was. He claimed Auburn couldn't afford to pay two coaches to do one job, and there were no dollars to spare.

The next stop was Governor Gordon Persons, an Auburn alumnus who applied pressure on President Draughon and the faculty athletic committee for a change. Draughon refused to budge, and the question seemed at an impasse. The athletic committee agreed Coach Brown would return for the 1951 season and Persons backed off.

A month later, though, the committee met again and surprised everyone by announcing Coach Brown had been fired and a search for a replacement would start immediately.

Shortly after the search began, athletic director Wilbur Hutsell decided to step down and return to coaching track. Jeff Beard, the athletic department's business manager, was named the new athletic director.

Beard and the search committee narrowed their focus to Shug Jordan, then on Coach Wally Butts' staff at the University of Georgia as offensive line coach and head basketball coach. Beard and Jordan had been friends since their days as Auburn students in 1932.

Jordan signed a five-year contract for $11,000 a year and began to assemble a staff. He retained three members of the previous coaching staff, all veteran Auburn men. Joel Eaves would coach defensive ends, serve as head scout, and continue as head basketball coach. Cary Lamar "Shot" Senn, who had been on the staff since 1944, would be offensive line coach and academic counselor. Dick McGowan was to coach the freshman football team and head the baseball program.

Jordan's hand-picked staff had a strong University of Georgia flavor. Homer Hobbs, an All-American guard at Georgia and a veteran of the NFL with the Forty-Niners and Redskins, was hired as an offensive line coach. George "Buck" Bradberry, a former Georgia running back, took over the defensive backfield. Buck came from Oklahoma State, where he served under J.B. "Ears" Whitworth, who would later become Alabama's head coach.

Gene Lorendo, who had led the SEC in pass receiving in 1949, would coach the offensive ends and be the resident manager of the Graves Center housing facility. His former Georgia teammate, Joe Connally, a coach at Decatur High School in Atlanta at the time, came over as a defensive line coach. Charlie Waller, who played at Oglethorpe College and was the head coach at Decatur High, was the new backfield coach. Waller later became head coach of the San Diego Chargers and was the first former Auburn coach to be the head coach of an NFL team.

Gene Lorendo and Senn could have been termed the "coaches of discipline" as Jordan's front men when a player screwed up. The two usually handled discipline problems, but occasionally one had to be referred to "The Man," Coach Jordan himself. No player wanted to face "The Man."

Auburn University Coaching Staff, 1951. First row: Homer Hobbs, Charlie Walker, Buck Bradberry. Second row: "Shot" Senn, Gene Lorendo, Ralph Jordan, Joel Eaves, and Dick McGowan. Not pictured: Joe Connally.

Kenny Howard remained as trainer for all Auburn athletes, serving throughout Jordan's twenty-five year tenure. Howard had been associated with Auburn athletics since 1948. Later in his career he served as a top trainer for the USA Olympic team. Kenny and Joe Connally lived in Graves Center and assisted Lorendo in the day-to-day operations of the facility, where the scholarship athletes resided.

The staff had to hit the ground running when they all got to Auburn. They had a lot of work ahead to become competitive in the

Southeastern Conference, but they had confidence in Jordan as a strong leader and rallied around him. Their first job, according to Shug, was "To put a foundation in the Auburn football program."

While Gene and his co-coaches were building that foundation, Gene's family was also building a life in Auburn. Jane had her hands full with the two boys, two-year-old Cam and Mac, who was less than a month old when the family moved to Auburn, and in April 1954, the family expanded one more time with the birth of a daughter, Leah.

Not long after Leah was born, Jane also began working on a master's degree in home economics (now human sciences) at Auburn, completing it in 1958. Jane then went to work at Auburn, teaching courses in ceramics, weaving, textile design, and pottery classes. Her imagination, creativity, and insight, coupled with her warmth and concern for others and her capacity to always provide praise and encouragement, endeared her to her students and colleagues.

Thankfully, as busy as Gene and Jane were, they had a whole team of babysitters at their disposal as the children grew up, among them football players Lloyd Nix, Tommy Lorino, Jimmy Morrow, and Joe Dolan, who all lived in nearby cabins. They also had a number of hoops players in the babysitting entourage including Jimmy Lee, Terry Chandler, Henry Hart, Ty Samples, and Rex Frederick, who recalled playing games with the Cam and Mac, both of whom proved to be exceptional escape artists.

The Smoking Box

Butch Bradberry, Buck's wife, remembered that Jane Lorendo did not allow Gene to smoke inside their Graves Center cottage and she had Gene leave his beloved cigars and pipes in a metal box on the front porch. Later, I found out from Kenny Howard that the metal smoking box was actually their mailbox.

As one of Jane's friends noted, Gene was the offensive coordinator of the Auburn football team, but Jane was the coordinator of the Lorendo home.

A Campfire Conversation with Lorendo

LORENDO

One winter night, Gene Lorendo was sitting around the campfire at Graves Center Amphitheater with several football players and managers when someone asked Lorendo about his earlier life growing up on the Mesabi Range.

Gene reminisced and seemed to be reflecting back on his time there in the '20s and '30s when he said, "Times were tough."

He recalled how his father, who eked out a living for his family as a drayman and constable, sometimes did not have enough money to pay the bills. When the bill collectors called, Gene Sr. would explain: At the first of the month he placed all their bills in his hat, then he pulled the bills out one by one. If your bill was one of the first selected, you would be paid. If not, your bill would go back in the hat for the next month.

CHAPTER NINETEEN:

LORENDO'S FIRST YEARS AT AUBURN

In their initial season on the Plains, Coach "Shug" Jordan and his new staff faced a huge challenge in their first game. Their opponent was Vanderbilt University, which had defeated Auburn 41-0 the previous season.

With Allen Parks at quarterback for Auburn, the Tigers upset Vanderbilt and their star quarterback, Bill Wade (who would later become a star player for the Chicago Bears in the NFL), 24-14 in their first game at Auburn in 1951. Auburn went on to win five of its first six games, losing only to an old nemesis, Georgia Tech, and then the wheels came off as they lost the last four games by sizeable margins.

This first Jordan-coached team had some notable players such as Vince Dooley, Bobby Freeman, George Atkins, "Blind" Bill Turnbeaugh, Jimmy Long, Bobby Duke, Lee Hayley, and Joe Davis. But it was obvious to Jordan and his coaching staff that they could not make "chicken salad without the chicken," and Auburn simply did not have enough quality players to win in the SEC. So Shug sent his coaches out to recruit some of the best football players in the South.

The coaches went to Birmingham, Atlanta, Montgomery, Mobile, and anywhere they could to find a good football player. Once they found a potential recruit, they had to convince him to come to the "Loveliest Village of the Plains" in Auburn, Alabama.

The 1952 season got off to a bad start when Auburn lost their first game to a highly ranked Maryland team 13-7. The Tigers would only win three games, with their best win being Clemson 3-0 (Clemson had defeated Auburn the previous year 34-0).

The Raffle

In the off season, a civic club in Auburn had a big raffle to raise money for a worthy charity. Raffle tickets were sold for one dollar, and Mac Lorendo, Gene's son, said his dad waited until the last day to buy a raffle ticket with the hope that his ticket would be drawn first. If your ticket was drawn, the challenge was to take a wheelbarrow out to the middle of the football field on the 50-yard line, lift and load a large cloth bag of coins weighing more than 100 pounds into the wheelbarrow, then roll the wheelbarrow off the playing field without the wheelbarrow tipping over.

If you have ever handled a wheelbarrow full of concrete mix you understand the challenge of pushing a wheelbarrow loaded with over 100 pounds of coins. And this was a small wheelbarrow. The bag was full of coins—pennies, nickels, dimes, quarters, half dollars, and a few silver dollars—valued at more than $800.

You had to be present when your raffle ticket was drawn to have a chance to win. Two men had their raffle tickets drawn before Lorendo. Both men were unable to lift the bag of coins and place the bag in the wheelbarrow without tipping the wheelbarrow over, thus disqualifying them from winning the prize money. Then they called Lorendo's number. He just smiled, walked out to the center of the football field, grabbed the bag of coins, placed it in the wheelbarrow, and rolled the wheelbarrow off the field without a problem.

Prior to the 1953 season, Coach Jordan hired Hal Herring, an Auburn man, as defensive coordinator. Herring, who had played linebacker for the Cleveland Browns under the famous Coach Paul Brown, was a brilliant defensive coach. Some say he was one of the best at adjusting a defense during a game. The Auburn defense started to play better and tougher under Coach Herring.

During 1953, Auburn started to show signs of improvement as a football team. With Bobby Freeman, Vince Dooley, Jim Pyburn, Joe Childress, Fob James, and Dave Middleton leading the way, the

Tigers finished with seven wins, two losses, and one tie. The biggest game of the year for Auburn was against Mississippi State when they were down 21 to 0 at the half, but came back to tie the game 21-21. Jim Pyburn, one of Lorendo's offensive ends, had a great game and an excellent season. Auburn was invited to the Gator Bowl, which they lost to Texas Tech.

After the 1954 season in which Auburn had an 8-3 season, two significant changes took place on the Auburn football team. First, Auburn's All-American end candidate, Jim Pyburn, who had one more year of eligibility as a college player, left to sign with the Baltimore Orioles for a reported $50,000 bonus. Second, Coach Charlie Waller left Auburn and took the job as the top offensive coach at Clemson. (From Clemson he would have a brief stop at Texas before joining the San Diego Chargers.) Homer Hobbs also left and took a job as an assistant coach at the Naval Academy.

When the assistant coaches were dressing for spring practice the next season, one of them reported that he had heard a rumor that Jeff Beard, Auburn's athletic director, was not going to replace Coach Waller on the staff. Instead, the rumor was that Beard was going to split up Coach Waller's salary and give all the assistant coaches a raise. The coaches were back dressing for practice a month later when the same coach said he finally got the scoop on the Coach Waller deal. Everyone's ears perked up. He said, "Hell! Coach Waller was working for nothing."

Auburn went to the Gator Bowl again in 1954, defeating Baylor. In 1955, Auburn won eight games and tied one. The big wins were over Georgia Tech, a team Auburn had not beaten since 1940, and Alabama. In the Georgia Tech game, Jerry Elliott and Jimmy "Red" Phillips, both offensive ends under Coach Lorendo, made big catches on the winning drive as Auburn won by a score of 14-12. In 1956, George Atkins and Vince Dooley joined the coaching staff.

That same year, the Auburn Tigers added a new name to their roster, a player who proved to be pivotal for the team: Tommy Lorino.

Lorino, a tailback who, in 1954, scorched the South as one of its hottest recruits, having led his Bessemer High School team to the

Alabama State Championship. Colleges from all over were interested in Lorino, with Georgia Tech apparently the early leader. (Coach Bobby Dodd had previously lured an impressive slate of former Bessemer players to his Yellow Jackets team. These included scatback Jimmy Thompson and All-Americans Don Stephenson and Maxie Baughan.)

Gene Lorendo, who drew the assignment to attract Lorino to Auburn's program, took an interesting approach to the task: He recruited the entire Lorino family. Gene became a frequent Thursday visitor for the family's special pasta night and he developed a close relationship with Tommy's father, so when it came time for Tommy to decide, Mr. Lorino's input was, "I think you should sign with Coach Lorendo and Auburn." Thus, the Tigers gained the prized signature.

However, the process was not quite final. Professional baseball tendered Lorino a substantial cash bonus, very attractive to Tommy, who was interested in playing pro baseball. Again Lorino's father stepped in. "I want you to go to Auburn and be the first in our family to have a college degree," he stated. That settled it.

Tommy Lorino, a prize Gene Lorendo recruit, and his teammates indeed distinguished themselves throughout their Auburn football careers and helped build that much-needed foundation that would carry Auburn football into a winning future. Lorino started at halfback for the Tigers in 1956, '57, and '58. His 8.4 yards per carry in '56 led the nation and set an SEC record. In addition, he punted for Auburn those three years and played stellar defense in an era when players were required to play both ways.

Auburn and Georgia Brawling

Gene Lorendo, like his father before him, was a "big, strong, and powerful man," a fact further illustrated when the 1956 Georgia-Auburn football game was played in Columbus, Georgia. A fight broke out during the game on the field, which was in horrible condition after a week of rain—more like a hog pen or a quagmire than a football playing field. As the Auburn and Georgia players were brawling, the game officials could not stop the fighting. But Coach Lorendo strolled out as the band played the national anthem and waded into the action, tossing players from both teams aside until he reached the middle. Then he placed both of his huge arms out and the fight was over. Lorendo was a giant of a man.

CHAPTER TWENTY:

THE FOUNDATION PAYS OFF WITH A NATIONAL CHAMPIONSHIP IN 1957

It appeared that all of the pieces of the puzzle were finally in place for the Auburn Tigers football team in 1957. Then, just before the start of the season, Coach "Shug" Jordan made an announcement: Two top players had been dismissed from the team—the starting quarterback and a linebacker. This decision shook up the whole team. Everyone received the message loud and clear. There would be discipline on the team. No exceptions!

After this announcement, Auburn supporters were wondering who would be the starting quarterback for the 1957 team. Jordan and Coach "Buck" Bradberry, the offensive backfield coach, tapped Lloyd Nix, a junior halfback who had played quarterback in high school at Carbon Hill, Alabama, to be the starting quarterback. Lloyd, a southpaw, had been moved to halfback during his freshman year at Auburn.

The coaches knew Lloyd Nix was a leader, a talented player, and a great competitor. Lloyd would lead the 1957 Auburn team to the national championship.

The team had a number of talented players including: Jimmy "Red" Phillips and Jerry Wilson, two great ends. The position coaches for these two outstanding ends were Coach Lorendo on offense and Coach Joel Eaves on defense. Phillips, an All-American, would go on to be an All-Pro player with the Los Angeles Rams. Wilson was a terrific pass rusher and run-stopper who played with the Philadelphia Eagles and San Francisco 49ers in the NFL and one season with the Toronto Argonauts of the

Canadian Football League, though bad ankles kept Wilson from having a great pro career. Both he and Phillips were All-SEC players.

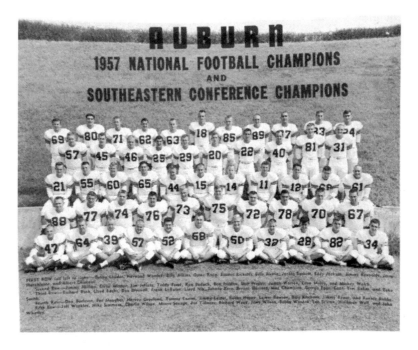

Auburn's 1957 National Championship Team.

The Tigers had a lot of great players on this championship team including center Jackie Burkett, guard Zeke Smith (both All-Americans; Zeke was the Outland Trophy winner), two top running backs in Tommy Lorino and Bobby Hoppe, and a tough fullback in Billy "Ace" Atkins. Tim Baker, a guard and captain, plus four strong tackles—Ben Preston, Dan Pressley, James Warren, and Cleve Webster—rounded out the team.

The first game of the year let everyone know Auburn was for real. Auburn had been crushed in 1956 by Tennessee and their All-American tailback, Johnny Majors, in a 35-7 loss in Birmingham. The following year (1957) in Knoxville, the Tigers dominated in the mud, winning 7-0 to open the season. The Auburn defense was the best in the country, giving up only seven points in Southeastern Conference play and a total of twenty-eight points for the entire season, finishing with a climactic 40-0 rout of their archrival, the Alabama Crimson Tide.

Coach Lorendo and Coach Joel Eaves with Auburn's two great ends: Jerry Wilson, All SEC, and Jimmy "Red" Phillips, All American.

When Shug Jordan and his coaching staff took over in 1951, Auburn had not won a single game the previous (1950) season and was on the bottom of the Southeastern Conference. The previous head coach had said no one could win at Auburn, but in seven years Coach Jordan and his staff had turned the football program completely around and guided the Tigers to the 1957 national championship, ending the season ranked as the No. 1 team in the nation by the Associated Press.

143

THE 1958 & '59 SEASONS

The defending national champions, the Auburn Tigers, opened the 1958 season on television with Tennessee in Birmingham, the first-ever televised game for Auburn. How good was Auburn's defense? The Volunteers failed to make a first down in the game. Tennessee finished the game with minus forty-nine yards rushing and the Tigers won 13-0.

That first game set the stage for another great year for Auburn, which ended without a single loss and only a 7-7 tie with Georgia Tech. In the last game of the year, Auburn defeated "Bear" Bryant's Alabama team 14-8 for the Tigers fifth straight win over Bama. Auburn had not lost in twenty-four straight games, the '58 team led the Southeastern Conference in total offense, and many Auburn fans thought the Tigers should have been the national champs again.

Auburn Coaching Staff, 1958. First row: Vince Dooley, Joel Eaves, "Shot" Senn, Shug Jordan, Hal Herring, Gene Lorendo, Buck Bradberry. Second row: Joe Connally, Dick McGowan, Erk Russell, and George Atkins.

That was not to be, though, because LSU, led by their great back Billy Cannon, was undefeated and won the national championship. Auburn finished fourth in the final AP poll and could not play in a bowl game again due to NCAA probation.

In 1959, Auburn finally lost a game when Tennessee edged the Tigers 3-0 in a hard-fought game in Knoxville. This Auburn team was led by two of Auburn's greatest players—Ken Rice, a tackle from Bainbridge, Georgia, who was an All-American for both the 1959 and '60 seasons, and Ed Dyas, an All-American fullback and field goal kicker from Mobile.

After this loss, Auburn bounced back with six straight victories before meeting Georgia in a big game for the Southeastern Conference championship in Athens. The Tigers were leading by a score of 13-7 with two minutes left in the game. Auburn had the ball and just needed a first down to run out the clock for the victory. The Tigers fumbled and Pat Dye, Georgia's All-American guard and future Auburn head coach, recovered for the Bulldogs. Fran Tarkenton, who would become a great NFL quarterback, threw a touchdown pass on fourth down with thirty seconds left for the victory. Final score: Georgia 14-Auburn 13.

Auburn finished the 1959 season ranked fourteenth in the nation. Though it was a far cry from their previous two years of success, there was no doubt Auburn's football program was a force to be reckoned with.

Because Auburn was placed on probation for illegal recruiting inducements by the NCAA for the 1957, '58, and '59 seasons, television and post-season bowl games were banned. (The probation stemmed from the recruitment of the Beaube twins, running backs from Gadsden, Alabama, whose father was a minister and supposedly turned Auburn in to the NCAA.)

A couple of seasons later, Auburn was back on probation in a case related to Don Fuell, an All-American quarterback from Guntersville, Alabama, who was the center of a big recruiting battle between Auburn and Alabama in 1957. Don signed a grant-in-aid to play at Auburn, but after an investigation by the NCAA, Fuell was suspended from playing in the SEC and Auburn was barred from playing in a bowl game through 1961. Don Fuell later signed with Southern Mississippi.

The Race

Bill Van Dyke was a highly sought-after high school football player from North Fulton High School in Atlanta. He cast his lot with Auburn because it was the right distance from home and Coach Jordan impressed him as a true southern gentleman. Van Dyke was a two-time All-SEC guard who lettered for the Tigers in 1962, '63, and '64 and played in the 1963 Orange Bowl against Nebraska.

During his playing days, Van Dyke and Coach Lorendo were known to have a few words back and forth in jest. One day Lorendo said to Van Dyke, "I can outrun your ass." Van Dyke took up the challenge.

The race was promoted for several days. Finally the day came to "put up or shut up." The race would be for forty yards. All of the players were pulling for Van Dyke and urging him on to victory. The assistant coaches were yelling words of encouragement for Lorendo.

Lorendo won the race by one step.

Van Dyke told me years later he was running with full pads without his helmet, while Lorendo was running with shorts and a tee-shirt. Van Dyke said, "I would have won if I had been in shorts."

Bill's dad was executive chef at Rich's Tea Room, one of the most popular luncheon spots in Atlanta during the latter part of the 1900s. He followed his dad to Rich's where he learned to carve ice and also met his wife, Nina Lowery. Later, he took up ice carving as a full-time occupation. Today, he is considered to be one of the most skilled ice carvers in the country. Eagles, tigers, bulldogs, falcons, hawks, or whatever you want, he can do it. He has carved for the Rolling Stones, Paul McCartney, Lisa Minnelli, and many other famous people.

CHAPTER TWENTY-ONE:

AUBURN FOOTBALL IN THE '60S

The 1960s for the most part was a winning decade of football for Auburn. The 1963 team turned out to be a fun team to watch as they won nine games, losing only to Mississippi State on a field goal with thirty seconds left to play. They defeated Alabama 10-8 to finish a successful season.

Jimmy Sidle, the Auburn quarterback, ran for a record 1,006 yards for the season, the only quarterback in Auburn history at this time to gain over a thousand yards. With Tucker Frederickson and Larry Rawson leading the blocking on end sweeps, Sidle was able to run for big gains. (Almost fifty years later Cam Newton ran for over 1,473 yards in the 2010 national championship season, and Nick Marshall added his name to the list in 2013 with 1,068 yards while leading Auburn to the national championship game.)

In addition to Sidle and Frederickson, who played both as a running back on offense and safety on defense, that year's team also boasted a roster of other outstanding players such as Bill Cody, Howard Simpson, Chuck Hurston, Larry Rawson, and George Rose.

That Auburn team was invited to play Nebraska in the 1963 Orange Bowl, which the Cornhuskers won 13-7 with a late Auburn drive failing at the goal line. The final AP poll had Auburn ranked fifth in the country.

All Auburn fans were excited and looking forward to the 1964 season. With Jimmy Sidle returning along with Frederickson in the backfield, Auburn would have two potential All-Americans to lead the team. Sidle, one of the leading candidates for the Heisman Trophy award, made the cover of *Sports Illustrated* in the preseason, and Auburn was picked by some as the No. 1 one team in the country. But Auburn's hopes were dashed in the first game, a 30-0 win over Houston, when Sidle severely injured his shoulder and would have difficulty passing the football for the remainder of the season.

Auburn finished the season with a 6-4 record. Had Sidle not been injured, Auburn would have had two strong Heisman Trophy candidates in Jimmy Sidle and Tucker Frederickson. If...if...if Jimmy Sidle had not been injured in the first game of the season in 1964, Auburn might have won another national championship and their first Heisman, which that year went to John Huarte, the quarterback of No. 3-ranked Notre Dame, which had a 9-1 record.

Huarte was taken in the sixth round of the NFL draft as the seventy-sixth pick. Who was the first player taken in the NFL draft? Tucker Frederickson of Auburn. And he was not the only Auburn player to make it into the pros that year. In the summer of 1964, Howard Simpson, one of Lorendo's outstanding ends, and teammate George Rose, a halfback, both signed with the Minnesota Vikings.

The Vikings held their summer training camp up in Bemidji, Minnesota, which was thirty miles south of the Lorendo's summer vacation cabin at Northome, Minnesota, so Coach Lorendo got to reconnect with his boys when he made a special trip down to Bemidji that summer to watch the Vikings practice, then Simpson and Rose returned the visit up to Lorendo's cabin on Island Lake.

THE 1968 TENNESSEE GAME AND MIKE CURRIER

November 9, 1968: The fifth-ranked Tennessee Vols met the eighteenth-rated Auburn Tigers in a big football game at Legion Field in Birmingham. Tennessee had one of the best defensive teams in college football, led by All-American linebackers Steve Kiner and Jack "Hacksaw" Reynolds.

Auburn's offensive coordinator, Gene Lorendo, had developed a special game plan that called for one of Auburn's smallest players, Mike Currier, who hailed from Oneonta, Alabama, to make big plays in the matchup of these highly ranked teams.

And just as Coach Lorendo had schemed, Mike Currier scored three touchdowns on his first four plays in the ball game. On his first play in the game, Mike caught an eleven-yard touchdown pass from quarterback, Loran Carter. In the second quarter he reentered the game with Auburn on the Tennessee 10-yard line. He ran a dive play down to the 2-yard line, and on the same dive play he scored his second touchdown.

Later in the second quarter, Loran Carter again found Mike Currier in the end zone for fourteen yards and a third TD. Auburn led fifth ranked Tennessee 21-0 and Mike Currier had scored all three touchdowns.

Tennessee bounced back in the game with quarterback Bubba Wyche, who threw for 337 yards, as he led the Vols with two touchdown drives to get Tennessee back in the game. Auburn sealed the victory in the fourth quarter with another touchdown pass from Loran Carter to All-SEC wide receiver Tim Christian for forty-nine yards and a final score of 28-14.

In a newspaper writeup of the game, some of the Tennessee defensive players commented they had difficulty finding the smaller Currier when he ran the ball or caught a pass. Tennessee only had one yard rushing for the entire game against the Auburn defense led by All-American defensive tackle David Campbell and linebackers, Mike Kolen and Ron Yarbrough, who shut down the Vols' running game.

According to Mike Currier, Coach Lorendo was one of the first coaches in the SEC to use three wide-outs in a game and was a brilliant offensive coach who was way ahead of his time as an offensive coordinator. Mike added that Lorendo would have loved Coach Malzahn's spread offense of the 2013 season; Coach Lorendo also liked to spread the field and stretch the defense.

Mike, who today is in the fracking business and travels often to Central America for his work, and Lorendo remained close through the years and, when Mike received word that Lorendo was dying, he called the coach to let him know he was thinking of him. Mike said, "We were good buddies."

CHAPTER TWENTY-TWO:

THE SULLIVAN-BEASLEY ERA AND THE GATOR BOWL

On a fall night in 1967, Kess Fabian, a '59 graduate of Auburn and a sales executive for McWane Cast Iron Pipe, had arranged to meet Coach Gene Lorendo in Birmingham, Alabama. Fabian was a member of a group of alumni who assisted the Auburn coaches in recruiting prospective high school football players in the Birmingham area, and on this night Fabian and Coach Lorendo planned to see a game between two top high schools, Shades Valley and John Carroll.

On one side of the field would be John Carroll, a private Catholic high school and a young and upcoming football team. John Carroll would later produce some Auburn stars such as Pat Sullivan, Tom Banks, Dick Schmalz, and Thom Gossom.

On the other side of the field, Coach Lorendo was actively recruiting Alvin Bressler of Shades Valley, who was one of the top wide receivers in the state of Alabama. Bressler, at six-two and 175 pounds, was also one of the elite sprinters and hurdlers in the South. Lorendo felt Bressler would bring a lot of speed to the Auburn offense and give the Tigers a deep threat as a pass receiver.

Lorendo and the Auburn coaching staff had also been hearing a lot of good reports on the John Carroll's young quarterback, Pat Sullivan, so this game would give Lorendo an opportunity to see both Bressler and Sullivan in action on the same field.

Both players performed at a high level in the game, and Lorendo was impressed with each of them. Lorendo and Fabian went down on the field after the game to speak with and congratulate the players.

As Fabian and Lorendo were leaving the stadium, Lorendo made a brash comment: "I am going to recruit Pat Sullivan next year, and I am going to sign him to a scholarship with Auburn. Pat will be an All-American quarterback and will win the Heisman." Fabian, who was driving, almost ran off the road.

The following Monday, Coach Lorendo excitedly reported to "The Man" (Coach Jordan) and the Auburn coaching staff at their weekly staff meeting, "I have found the quarterback who can lead Auburn to victory in the future. He is Pat Sullivan at John Carroll High School in Birmingham."

Once he had seen Sullivan play, Lorendo's major objective and assignment was to recruit Pat to sign a football scholarship with Auburn. He was fully aware Coach "Bear" Bryant and his staff at Alabama were also recruiting Sullivan.

During these years, Coach Bryant would sign six or more quarterbacks each year. Since a good high school quarterback was usually one of the best athletes on their high school team, a number of these quarterbacks were then moved to other positions, such as defensive back or wide receiver. Auburn fans thought the Bear signed some of those quarterbacks just to keep them from signing with Auburn.

While Coach Lorendo was going all out in a battle with Alabama to sign Pat Sullivan, another major recruiting battle was brewing down in Montgomery. Terry Beasley at Robert E. Lee High School was one of the best wide receivers in the nation. Tom Jones, the Auburn freshman football team coach and the former coach of Lee High School in Montgomery, was given the task of recruiting and signing Beasley, who was also a high school track star with blinding speed. He had won the 100- and 200-yard dashes in the Alabama state track championship.

Alabama had dominated the state in recruiting most of the years Coach Bryant was at Alabama. Now, with Pat Sullivan leaning to Auburn, the Tide did not want to lose another top prospect to Auburn. When Terry Beasley visited Alabama, Coach Bryant, his staff, and the Alabama team did everything they could to get a commitment from Terry.

In the summer after their senior year, Pat Sullivan and Terry Beasley played on the same team in the Alabama high school all-star game, during which Pat threw three touchdown passes to Terry, and they developed a close friendship. After Pat Sullivan committed to Auburn, Terry Beasley made the decision to join Sullivan and the Auburn Tigers.

With the signing of Pat Sullivan and Terry Beasley, plus a good overall recruiting class, Auburn fans were excited with their potential for the coming seasons.

The next fall, everyone was watching closely as the Auburn freshman team traveled to Tuscaloosa to meet the Alabama freshman team. The first score that was announced over the wire was Alabama 27-0 in the first half. Well, so much for hope! Then a little glimmer of hope came across the wire. Auburn had cut the lead in the first half to 27-15 with a thirty-three-yard touchdown pass from Pat Sullivan to Daryl Johnson and a thirty-six-yard TD pass to Terry Beasley.

In the second half, Sullivan connected with Beasley again for seventy-two yards to cut the lead to 27-22. Auburn then stopped Alabama in four plays. Auburn took possession, but after not gaining any yardage in three plays, it appeared the Tigers would be forced to give the ball back to Bama. David Beverly came in on fourth down to punt, but crossed up Alabama by faking the punt and running sixteen yards for a first down.

Sullivan and company took over and drove the Tigers to the end zone and the lead, 29-27. But Auburn was not through. After stopping Alabama, Sullivan passed to Beasley for thirty-eight yards and the Tigers punched it in for the touchdown and the final score of 36-27. Hope was alive again for the future of the Auburn football program.

The era of Pat Sullivan and Terry Beasley was an exciting time for Auburn fans. With Sullivan at quarterback and an outstanding group of receivers in Beasley, Dick Schmalz, Connie Frederick, Alvin Bressler, and tight end Ronnie Ross, Lorendo was able to employ a wide-open offense. The addition of running backs Mickey Zofko, Wallace Clark, and Tommy Lowry, gave the Tigers an even more potent offense.

Coach Lorendo with All-Americans Pat Sullivan and Terry Beasley.

The highlights of the 1969 season were big victories over Clemson (51-0), Georgia Tech (17-14), Florida (38-12), Georgia (16-3), and last but not least, Alabama (49-26). To beat Alabama and Bear Bryant by three touchdowns was huge. The Tigers capped off their victory with a spectacular eighty-five-yard touchdown run by punter Connie Frederick.

The biggest disappointment of that season was the 20-21 loss to LSU. Auburn drove ninety-five yards in the fourth quarter to score and get within one point, only then to have the extra point blocked.

The 1970 season also proved to be an exciting season for the Auburn Tigers. With Sullivan throwing to Beasley and Schmaltz,

Auburn had two of the best receivers in college football. This team would become the highest scoring team in Auburn history.

In the first big game of the season, Auburn defeated Tennessee 36-23 in Birmingham. The next game was a two-fold victory over Georgia Tech. The score was 31-7, but the fact that this was the first time Georgia Tech had played at Cliff Hare Stadium in Auburn for more than twenty-five years was a second reason to celebrate.

Next came one of the most one-sided wins in Auburn history as the Tigers thrashed Florida by the score of 63-14. There were so many big plays in this game it is almost hard to imagine. To start with, Terry Beasley had three touchdowns, two coming on TD passes (eighty and seventeen yards, respectively) from Sullivan and another on a thirty-four-yard end-around play. James Owens, an up-and-coming player with star potential, capped the scoring off with an eighty-nine-yard punt return for a touchdown.

That same year, Georgia slipped up on Auburn to upset the Tigers 31-17, after which Auburn had to face Bear Bryant and his Alabama Crimson Tide in their next game. Alabama could not forget that Auburn had beaten them the year before by twenty-three points and this was another shootout at Legion Field in Birmingham. But the Tigers again defeated the Tide with a score of 35-28. This loss was a bitter defeat for Bryant and his Bama team, giving Pat Sullivan and Terry Beasley a 3-0 record against the mighty Alabama Crimson Tide.

THE 1970 GATOR BOWL AND SPENCE MCCRACKEN

Spence McCracken, who had played high school football on the powerful teams at Robert E. Lee High School in Montgomery, received a football scholarship to Auburn in 1967 and went on to letter as a center in 1969, '70, and '71.

After graduation from Auburn, he returned to his high school alma mater to become an outstanding coach at Robert E. Lee High School where he won three Alabama high school state championships and was named Coach of the Year by *USA Today* in

1986. (Later, he continued his success as head coach at Opelika High School, just down the road from Auburn.)

Having played for Lorendo during Auburn's glory days in the early 1970s, Spence had several good Lorendo stories.

Among them was a fall day when Spence had dressed early for Auburn football practice and was sitting out on a bench near the practice field. He was enjoying the scenery of coeds walking by on their way to classes, wishing he could join them rather than go out to practice in the ninety-plus degrees of heat and stifling humidity.

About that time Terry Beasley, Auburn's All-American wide receiver, walked by in his street clothes. Spence and Terry were good buddies and had attended high school together in Montgomery, so Spence said to Beasley, "Where are you going Terry?" Beasley replied, "I'm not feeling well. I'm going back to my dorm room in Sewell Hall."

A few minutes, later Coach Lorendo came walking up and McCracken said to him, "Coach could I ask you a question? Beasley just walked by and said he was not going to practice today. Said he is not feeling well. Coach, how about me? I really don't feel like practicing today."

Lorendo looked at McCracken, smiled, and remarked, "Crack, Beasley is the franchise. You're a piece of shit." With some zest in his voice and a big smile, Lorendo continued, "Come on Crack, let's go practice."

Spence also recalled a game in 1970 when Auburn played Ole Miss in the Gator Bowl, a classic matchup with quarterbacks Archie Manning leading Ole Miss and Pat Sullivan leading Auburn. The most unusual fact of this bowl game was that neither of the head coaches could attend the game. Shug Jordan had undergone an emergency appendectomy and was instructed to remain at home in Auburn, while John Vaught, the famous head coach at Ole Miss, also had a medical problem and was back in Oxford, Mississippi.

Coach Paul Davis, the defensive coordinator who was the acting head coach for the Auburn Tigers during that game, got up and said a few words to the team in the pre-game meeting, then he called on Coach Lorendo.

In his deep booming voice, Lorendo said, "This is not a threat. This is a fact. If we don't win this game today, we will have the toughest winter workouts and spring practice in the history of Auburn football."

Following those words from Lorendo, Spence walked over to quarterback Pat Sullivan and receivers Terry Beasley and Dick Schmalz and said, "We have to win this game today."

Auburn did win in a great game 35-28 with 71,000 in attendance and Pat Sullivan was named the MVP of the Gator Bowl. He had finished his junior year as the leader of the nation in total offense. His name was mentioned along with other top candidates for the Heisman award, for which he finished sixth in the Heisman voting in 1970.

According to Spence, the workouts that winter and during the following spring practice were the easiest in his five seasons at Auburn. Coach Lorendo had kept his word.

CHAPTER TWENTY-THREE:

1971: THE HEISMAN SEASON

The 1971 season kicked off with a 60-7 warm-up win over Chattanooga. Then the big matchup with the ninth-ranked Tennessee Vols and a national television audience loomed ahead in Knoxville. Tennessee had not lost at home in five years and the Vols' fans were eagerly looking forward to this big game with the fifth-ranked Auburn Tigers and their Heisman Trophy candidate, quarterback Pat Sullivan.

With 63,000 fans in attendance, and most of them in Tennessee orange, it was a perfect setup for a major upset. An Auburn friend of mine and his wife attended that classic SEC battle in Knoxville, arriving early at the stadium just as the gates were opened, along with a number of the players' parents and Auburn supporters. They were on hand to watch the Auburn team as they did their traditional walk around the opponent's field before the game. The Tigers were sharply dressed in their blue blazers with orange and blue ties. The team captains for this game were leading the walk with Coach "Shug" Jordan and Coach Gene Lorendo bringing up the rear of the team.

Three or four hundred Tennessee students had also gathered early in the student section to cheer their team on to victory and, as the Auburn team walked by, the students jeered and yelled obscenities at the Auburn team—"Auburn eats shit. Auburn eats shit."

The team and Coach Jordan continued their walk into the visiting clubhouse room. Coach Lorendo stayed behind and walked over in front of the student section. As they continued to shout "Auburn eats shit," Lorendo stood silent in front of them until the crowd became quiet. Then he stepped forward and said, "Yes, and we will have Tennessee for lunch today."

The Tennessee game proved to be a traditional battle between two top teams. The Vols were leading with six minutes to play in the fourth quarter when Pat Sullivan gathered the offensive team in the huddle on their own 14-yard line and said, "We can win this game."

First was a pass to Terry Beasley, and then one to Dick Schmalz at the 43-yard line. Sullivan found Schmalz again at the Tennessee 35, then whom Sullivan fired a bullet pass to Beasley, and Terry sprinted down to the 15-yard line. Before the Vols could catch a breath, Pat passed to Schmalz again at the 6-yard line. From there, Auburn's Harry Unger ran it in for the winning touchdown: Auburn 10, Tennessee 9.

Auburn rolled on through their 1971 schedule beating Kentucky 38-6, Southern Mississippi 27-14, Georgia Tech 31-7, Clemson 35-13, Florida 40-7, and Mississippi State 30-21 before facing the unbeaten Georgia Bulldogs in Athens.

A lot was riding on this classic battle between two highly ranked and undefeated SEC teams. The Tigers and Bulldogs were playing for an undefeated season, a conference championship, a major bowl bid, and a possible national championship. The game was sold out and there was no television. Scalpers were having a field day, with the ticket prices rising daily.

According to Sullivan, on November 12 when the Auburn team in their two busses approached Athens, the Georgia students were out in numbers and they circled the busses ten to fifteen miles from town to let the Tigers know they were in Bulldog country. This was a sign of what was to take place later when they arrived at the Holiday Inn downtown. Pat said the team became very quiet as they rode into Athens.

When they arrived at Sanford stadium for their walk-thru practice, the Georgia students were there, letting the sixth-ranked Auburn Tigers and their Heisman Trophy candidate know they were in enemy territory. A white sheet sign with red letters could be seen at the top of the stadium that read, "Piss on Pat." The sign was removed the next day before the game.

The Holiday Inn in downtown Athens was near the campus and the fraternity houses. After the team had dinner and attended a movie, they returned to the Holiday Inn for the night. Sullivan said it was always difficult enough to sleep before a big game like Georgia, but the noise from the fraternity houses and the students was a major distraction, making sleep almost impossible. The Georgia students continued their noisy partying and loud music could be heard throughout the night.

On that Friday night before the big game between the No. 6-ranked Auburn Tigers and the No. 7-ranked Georgia Bulldogs, Coach Gene Lorendo and Auburn alumnus Kess Fabian attended a high school game in the Athens area to watch a highly touted running back, Horace King of Clark Central High School. Horace King would later sign with University of Georgia and then play in the NFL for several seasons.

As Lorendo and Fabian returned to the Athens Holiday Inn around 10:30 p.m. that night, they encountered a Georgia fan outside of the ground floor of the Holiday Inn where the team was staying. The fan was heckling the Auburn team yelling, "Where are the Auburn Tigers? I want to see Pat Sullivan and Terry Beasley. I want to see Sullivan and Beasley. Where are the Auburn Tigers?"

Coach Lorendo walked over to the fan and said, "Please keep the noise down. Our players are trying to get some rest." Apparently the fan gave a response that Lorendo did not appreciate. Lorendo started walking toward the Georgia fan who quickly retreated into his room. Before the heckler could lock the door, though, Lorendo pushed it open. The fan sought safety behind the locked door of the bathroom.

Gene said to the three women and two other men in the room, "Tell your friend in the bathroom if I hear another word from him, I am going to come back and kick his ass."

According to Kess, after Lorendo left the room the occupants quickly closed the drapes and locked the door. A few minutes later he observed the heckler pulling back the drapes enough to take a peek outside. They did not hear another word from the heckler the rest of the night.

It was cold and cloudy on the morning of November 13, 1971, but the sun came out by mid-morning, making it a beautiful fall day for a college football game. The stadium was packed with fans in every conceivable space—they were on the bridge, the grass bank in front of the train trestle, sitting on top of buildings with their legs hanging over the edge, some were even in large trees. Everyone wanted to see "The Game."

This was a matchup between Lorendo's powerful Auburn offense and Erk Russell's nationally ranked Georgia defense. Auburn was led by Pat Sullivan and his strong receiving corps of speedy Terry Beasley and the clutch receiving of Dick Schmalz, plus a trio of talented running backs in Tommy Lowry, Terry Henley, and Harry Unger.

Andy Johnson, a sophomore quarterback, was a developing star for the Bulldogs. Johnson would eventually become one of the leading rushing quarterbacks in Georgia history and the Southeastern Conference. Lorendo had tried to recruit the highly sought-after quarterback from Athens, Georgia (during Andy Johnson's recruitment by Lorendo, Pat Sullivan had been Johnson's host on his visit to Auburn), but Johnson ended up signing with Georgia.

Auburn, with their fast-striking offense, won the toss and promptly came down the field with Pat Sullivan running for fifteen yards, then going to the air with passes to Tommy Lowry and Dick Schmalz, who almost scored as he was pushed out of bounds on the 2-yard line. On the next play, Lowry took it in for the touchdown.

Before some fans were back in their seats, Auburn had stopped Georgia and had the ball back again. The Tigers had found something in their first drive throwing to Tommy Lowry out of the backfield and the Bulldogs were doubling their pass coverage on Terry Beasley, which left a linebacker on Lowry. Sullivan went back to Lowry again for ten yards. Next, Pat threw a quick pass to Schmalz for eighteen yards down to the Georgia 34. Now, with Georgia wondering where Sullivan would go next, he hit Terry

Beasley with a perfect strike for the touchdown. Garner Jett kicked the extra point and Auburn was up 14-0.

Just as the Auburn fans were feeling pretty good "between the hedges," Andy Johnson with two strong runs had moved Georgia from their 20-yard line down the field to the Tigers' 2-yard line. The Dogs scored and it was a 14-7 game. Georgia stopped the Tigers and they were back in business with back Jimmy Poulos and Andy Johnson doing the heavy work as they drove down the field to tie the game 14-14.

Auburn needed to regain the momentum in the second quarter. Starting from their own 35-yard line, Harry Unger had a couple of good runs before Sullivan hooked up with Beasley for fourteen yards. After a pass interference call, Sullivan threw fourteen yards to Dick Schmalz for the touchdown. Gardner Jett booted the extra point and Auburn led, 21-14.

The Auburn defense under Coach Paul Davis and his staff played Georgia tough all day. The Tigers were led by Captain Tommy Yearout at tackle, end Bob Brown, linebacker Bobby Strickland, and safety Johnny Simmons.

After a scoreless third quarter, Auburn fumbled on their 26-yard line and the Dogs recovered. Andy Johnson took it in quickly for the touchdown to cut the Tigers lead to 21-20. Georgia was about to get back in the game. The home crowd could smell an upset victory over the higher ranked Tigers and their Heisman Trophy candidate.

An extra point is almost automatic with a good kicker and Georgia had a fine one in Kim Braswell. But Auburn had a secret weapon in Roger Mitchell, a specialist at blocking kicks. The ball was snapped to the holder and Braswell moved forward to boot the extra point just as Mitchell made a lunge into the air with his arms extended. Roger somehow got a hand on the ball, and Auburn maintained the lead 21-20. This was a big point in this battle of unbeaten teams.

The Tigers now needed another touchdown to give them a little more cushion. James Owens ran the kickoff back to the Auburn 30-yard line. Everyone in the stadium knew Sullivan could hit Beasley with a bomb on any play, and the Georgia secondary was well aware of Beasley's speed. Georgia could not afford to let Beasley get behind them on a long pass. Pat Sullivan knew the Georgia secondary was playing back on their heels in coverage.

Sullivan threw a strike to Beasley on a crossing route underneath on the right side. Two Georgia defensive backs zeroed in on Beasley...bam...Terry was hit at the same time by the two defensive backs coming from opposite directions and he was sandwiched between them. The sound of the impact could be heard throughout the stadium.

For one second, time stood still. Was Terry injured? Was he out of the game? Then, amazingly, even though Beasley was staggering and trying to regain his balance, he somehow found his feet a yard away from the two Georgia defenders. Terry turned and started sprinting downfield. When Terry Beasley had a step on you, the race to the goal line was over. As he reached the 10-yard line, he held the ball up to signal the touchdown. Auburn was up 28-20 and had taken control of the game.

The Tigers added another touchdown for insurance after James Owens made a terrific sixty-yard punt return. Sullivan went back to his two great receivers, Beasley and Schmalz, the latter of which grabbed his second touchdown of the game to finish the scoring at 35-20. Beasley and Schmalz both had great days as they finished with two touchdown catches each.

Another plus in this big game for the Tigers was the punting by David Beverly, who averaged forty-seven yards on six punts.

Pat Sullivan had completed fourteen of twenty-four passes for 248 yards and four touchdowns. The four touchdown passes gave Sullivan a total of fifty-three in his career at Auburn, breaking the Southeastern Conference record for passing touchdowns, which was previously held by Babe Parilli of Kentucky.

After the game, Georgia's head coach Vince Dooley commented to the *Atlanta Journal*, "Sullivan is the best I have ever seen."

Sullivan had made his statement for the Heisman Trophy, though the announcement of the winner would not come until November 25th. At halftime of the Georgia-Georgia Tech game in Atlanta, on

Thanksgiving night, the announcement was made by Bud Palmer of ABC Sports in New York: "The 1971 Heisman Trophy winner is Pat Sullivan of Auburn University," an announcement that thrilled Auburn people everywhere.

When the Heisman Trophy ceremony was held in New York City, Coach Gene Lorendo, who had recruited Pat and was his offensive coordinator, was there in his tux to share in this special night of celebrating Pat Sullivan's selection.

Heisman Award Ceremony, 1971, New York City. Buddy Davidson, Auburn Sports Information Director, Coach Gene Lorendo, Offensive Coordinator, Tommy Yearout, Team Captain, and Shug Jordan, Head Coach.

One man who cannot be overlooked in this Heisman race of 1971 is Buddy Davidson, who was the Sports Information Director at Auburn. Buddy had a low-key approach to informing the Associated Press voters what Pat Sullivan had accomplished in his career at Auburn and how valuable he was to the success of the team.

The award was even more special for Auburn because its namesake, John Heisman, coached at Auburn University from 1895-1899. In his coaching career, Heisman also coached at Oberlin College from 1892-94, Clemson (1900-03), Georgia Tech (1904-19, during which time he won a national championship for Georgia Tech in 1917), University of Pennsylvania (1920-22), Washington & Jefferson College (1923), and Rice University (1924-27).

Auburn is the only one of the seven colleges where Heisman coached in his career to have a player win a Heisman Trophy, and Auburn has had three winners of the prestigious award: Pat Sullivan, Bo Jackson, and Cam Newton.

CHAPTER TWENTY-FOUR:

"IS THAT ALL YOU'VE GOT?"
THE BILL NEWTON STORY

Back in 1969, Auburn assistant football coach Sam Mitchell recruited brothers Bill and Bob Newton, both of whom were outstanding high school players at Fayette, Alabama, to play football at Auburn.

Bob was a big offensive lineman at 230 pounds. Bill was a guard and a linebacker at 185 pounds. When the time came to offer scholarships Coach Mitchell (who passed away in Athens, Georgia, in January of 2015) had only one scholarship and it was offered to Bob. Bill was invited to walk on at Auburn as a non-scholarship player.

When Bill arrived at Auburn as a walk-on, he was an undersized offensive lineman. At the end of his freshman year, he asked Coach Mitchell if he could change positions to linebacker.

When spring practice arrived, Bill found himself and other walk-on linebackers lining up to take on a first team offensive lineman in one-on-one drill, with a dummy on each side of the hole with a running back behind a big first team offensive lineman.

Bill Newton thought the purpose of the drill was for the walk-ons to get blocked or knocked on their tails. So, when Coach Lorendo motioned for him to take the defensive position across from a big starting offensive lineman, he allowed the offensive lineman to easily block him out of the way.

Lorendo came in cussing and hollering at Bill Newton: "Is that that all you've got?"

Bill's response to himself was…. "No, that's not all I've got!" The next time Newton came up in the rotation he made up his mind that he was not going to let the offensive lineman have his way. When the ball was snapped, Bill fired out under the big lineman, submarining him, knocking the lineman off balance, and making the tackle. Now Bill watched as the big first team lineman was on the receiving end of Lorendo's wrath and cussing.

That simple "Is that all you've got?" comment by Coach Lorendo resulted in Bill Newton's football career going from nowhere to becoming a legend in Auburn football history. Coach Lorendo's one-liner made a major impact on Bill Newton's future football career at Auburn.

Linebacker Bill Newton would later have one of the top individual performances in Auburn football history when he led the Tigers to an upset victory over No. 2-ranked Alabama.

Lorendo Family, Gene and Jane with children Cam, MacLean (Mac) and Leah

CHAPTER TWENTY-FIVE:

"THE BEST YOU CAN"

By David Housel; reprinted from *Auburn Football Illustrated* in fall of 1972

Just what do ballet and football have in common? You wouldn't be expected to know the answer to that one unless you happen to be like the Gene Lorendo family. They'd know. But then they might know something about most anything. They are versatile.

First, there's Papa, Gene, Auburn's offensive coordinator and war hero. Then there's Mamma, Jane, artist, outdoor-woman, and one of Auburn's outstanding professors. Then there are three children: Mac, good student, football captain, and All-SEC contender; next there is Cam, ballet dancer with, among others, the Harkness, and New York Ballet companies; and last, but certainly not least, there's Leah, a good student and a ballet and jazz dancer. It should come as no surprise then, that the Lorendos would know the common ground of ballet and football, but even they didn't know it until four years ago when Cam brought a friend from the North Carolina School of Arts home with him for the Tennessee game.

On the way to Birmingham, Cam was telling his friend, who had never seen a college football game, what to expect. "Well," he said, "To be honest, it's a lot like ballet. They do the same movements we do in warming up, and a lot of the body maneuvers on the field are similar to dance moves."

"Sure enough," laughs Mrs. Lorendo, "when Auburn began warming up, Cam and his friend began naming the dancing moves

171

one by one. The only difference," she says, "is that dancers do them to music while football players do them to cheers of thousands."

Mac leaves no doubts, however, that he would prefer making his moves on the football field. "It's a lot easier," he says. "Imagine doing this much exercise eight hours a day, 365 days a year. That's what Cam has to do, and that's work, brother, believe you me." Having a tackle and a ballet dancer in the house has been amusing for the Lorendos not from inside, but from outside.

People used to always ask, "Doesn't Gene wish Cam would cut his hair" or "Doesn't Gene wish Cam would play football," Mrs. Lorendo says laughing. "They'd always ask me, but never Gene. We would get a good laugh out of it."

"The truth is," she continued, "Gene is the one who talked Cam into wearing his hair longer. He told him that if his profession called for it, then he ought to do it." That philosophy was in keeping with the motto of the Lorendo household: "Whatever you do, do it to the best of your ability."

"Gene was real careful not to put any pressure on the boys to play football," their mother says. "He wouldn't even let the boys have a football for a long time. It was embarrassing when other children would come over to play and our boys didn't have a football. I had to talk him into letting them finally have one."

Talking Gene Lorendo into anything is not an easy task. Not only is he a good athlete and a football coach, but he was a tough soldier in World War II. He was one of the first Americans to land in Japan, four days before the war ended, and his daring delivery of sealed messages put him up for a Congressional Medal of Honor consideration.

If anyone had an easy time talking "Big Gene" into anything, however, Jane Lorendo would be the one. She has the knowledge and artistic touch. A former president of Auburn's chapter of Phi Kappa Phi, she was named one of Auburn's outstanding professors by students in the School of Home Economics where she taught a series of loom weaving and ceramics courses. She also loved the outdoors. Canoeing down the rivers of Minnesota, where they have *a cabin, was one of Mrs. Lorendo's favorite activities. Only Cam would go with her, however. "Gene is afraid of water," she laughed.*

Leah, the only daughter and the youngest of the Lorendos, is following the dancing footsteps of her brother Cam, but she loves athletics and is a talented lady.

Versatility has great advantages. For example, the family got together and built their own house several years ago, and that's versatility that pays, and saves.

CHAPTER TWENTY-SIX:

THE "AMAZINS"

January 2, 1972: As the sun came up in the east on the patio of the Hotel Fountainbleau in New Orleans, Coach Gene Lorendo lit his large Savinelli pipe, poured a cup of New Orleans's best Cajun coffee, and enjoyed the view of the French Quarter.

Auburn had lost to Oklahoma in the Sugar Bowl on the previous day (New Year's Day) 40 to 22. Oklahoma clearly had the superior team—as one of their rabid fans and supporters stated, it was, "The best team money could buy." And if you had the opportunity to see this fan, you would understand why it might be true. He was wearing a white, ten-gallon cowboy hat, a red Oklahoma Sooner shirt, and expensive cowboy boots. He was driving a beautiful pearl-white Cadillac with a tag on the front displaying a gushing oil well. He went on to say, "As long as these oil wells keep pumping, we will have a great team."

Lorendo sipped on his coffee and puffed on his pipe as he reflected on the 1971 Auburn season. The Tigers had won nine straight games with big wins over Tennessee on national television, followed by victories over Kentucky, Georgia Tech, Clemson, and Georgia. The Georgia game was classic, with Auburn winning in Athens 35-20 in a great game. And, to wrap the season up perfectly, Pat Sullivan had been named as the Heisman Trophy winner for 1971.

Now it was Lorendo's twentieth season at Auburn. Most assistant football coaches don't stay at one college for twenty years; At Auburn, we probably have had 200 assistant football coaches in the last twenty years. Lorendo knew the heart of his offense was graduating. In fact, approximately ninety-five percent of his offensive playmakers would be gone—Heisman Trophy winner Pat Sullivan, All-American wide receiver Terry Beasley, and a number of All-SEC players including wide receiver Dick Schmalz and outstanding linemen Tommy Yearout and Bob Brown.

The truth of the matter was, the Auburn offense was diminished and their prospects for a winning season in 1972 were at the very best extremely bleak. Why would Lorendo hang around for another season when he could walk away and retire at the top of his coaching career? Having been a part of the national championship coaching staff in 1957, coaching for a number of winning seasons, and then capping off his career with the 1971 team and a 9-2 record, the Sugar Bowl, and a Heisman Trophy, Lorendo could leave the program with his head held high and a feeling of accomplishment.

The only problem was, Gene Lorendo loved coaching—the career he had chosen way back during his days up in the Mesabi Range of northern Minnesota in 1939—and he wasn't about to back down from an almost impossible challenge and the 1972 season. Lorendo had always demanded that his players give Auburn one hundred percent when they were on the athletic field. And when they didn't give one hundred percent, he told the players that Auburn would be better off without them. Now he was facing a personal decision. Could he give Auburn 100 percent in a season when the prospects for winning were overwhelmingly stacked against him and Auburn?

Lorendo could not walk away from this tremendous challenge. He had always challenged his players. Now he was being challenged. Lorendo made the decision to stay and fight. He said, "We may not be the most talented team in the Southeastern Conference, but we can be the toughest."

A lot of stories have been written about the "field position football" played back in the 1940s. Well, Auburn and the '72 team were about to revert back to the field position football strategy of the forties. What was that strategy? It was really pretty simple. A solid defense and good kicking can keep you in the game. Then it comes down to field position. As an offensive player, your job or challenge is to move the ball down the field one inch, one foot, or one yard at a time, hopefully with a first down or two, inching closer to the opponent's goal line. Then, if the other team's defense stops you, your excellent punter backs the opposing team up even more. Shug Jordan told the '72 team, "We have one-third of the game won before the kickoff since we have an excellent kicking game."

That spring's practice was not a place for the weak at heart. According to those who had been around the Auburn football program for years, the winter workouts and spring practices were the toughest they had ever witnessed.

One of the first challenges was to find a quarterback. Dave Lyon, a letterman defensive back and former quarterback, was favored to be the starting quarterback. Dave Lyons had an excellent spring and the coaching staff was excited about his future as a quarterback and the leader of the offense.

No one can tell the story better than a player who was there. And Thom Gossom, Jr. was just such a player. This excerpt is taken from pages 109-111 of his excellent book:

Walk-On
My Reluctant Journey to Integration at Auburn University
By Thom Gossom, Jr.
Published by State Street Press and Best Gurl, Inc.

"It is still said to be the roughest winter workout and spring practice in Auburn football history. We had marathon practices; two and a half to three hours of constant hitting. Everybody blocked and tackled in savage drills. There were everyday scrimmages. First team offense against first team defense. Injured guys were dragged off the field.

Sherman Moon, a wingback on the 1972 team said, "We went back to a World War II coaching mentality. You had to prove your manhood every day. Sell out your body every day. They broke you down and remade you."

Discipline was our first D. We had to have our helmets on, with chinstrap fastened, the entire practice. No exceptions.

There was one water break per practice. There was no Gatorade or buckets of water. There was the same outdoor faucet, a foot off the ground.

Defense was the second D. We would have a good defense for the coming year. We had several starters back and several who had gotten considerable playing time. The offense would consist of young guys, vying for playing time. The coaches challenged us to an offense versus defense daily competition. Fights broke out almost every day. Many guys just walked off, called it quits.

"I quit twice," Ken Bernich tells me. "That spring was the most brutal thing I'd ever been through." A linebacker, Ken would become a starter on the '72 team and an All-American on the '74 team. "I packed a suitcase and walked to the bus station in town. Coach Davis pulled up in his car. 'You're not leaving,' he told me. I got in and came back."

Most scrimmages, we never threw a pass. It was just one run after another. The same play over and over. When guys bristled, the coaches didn't back down. Terry Henley says, "One day Coach Lorendo tried to run me to death. I ran the ball twenty something times in a row. He was testing me. I knew it. I wanted to prove to him I could stand what he could dish out.

I fumbled the ball a couple of times, a big no-no. He grabbed me. Spun me around. I balled up my fist. He got close to me and whispered, 'I know you want to hit me but if you do, I'm going to kill you.' Henley laughed, "That sort of took the edge off my wanting to hit him."

Near the end of a rough two and one-half hour practice with very little left in our tanks, we would do goal line drills. We'd start at the 10-yard line, first and goal. Full speed, first team offense against first team defense. We had four downs to score.

We offensive guys would break the huddle, run to the line of scrimmage. The defense awaited us. The quarterback, Dave Lyons, would bark signals. Coach Lorendo would step between the offense and defense.

"Point to that son of a bitch you're going to block," he'd command us. We knew the drill. We would point to the defender

we were going to block. "Tell him you're going to block him."
As the wing-back, my assignment was to double team the
defensive end with the offensive tackle. "We're going to block
you." We pointed to Danny Sanspree. Danny would make All-
Conference.

Coach Lorendo would take it further. "Tell them who's
getting the ball." We would turn and point to Henley.
"Henley's getting the ball," we'd say. "Tell them the play,"
Coach Lorendo would demand. "Twenty-Seven Slant," we'd
say. "Point to the hole he is running in." We would point to the
hole off the outside of the right tackle. Coach Lorendo had one
more thing he wanted us to tell the defense. "Tell them the snap
count." We'd tell them, "The snap count is on two."

Coach Lorendo would then back out of the way. Before
leaving he'd tell the offense, "You better score."

The 1972 season was looking good until, two days before A-Day
and the spring game, Dave Lyons, the starting quarterback, went
down with a career-ending knee injury. Four other quarterbacks
were on the roster: Joe Bruner of Fort Walton Beach, Florida, and
Alabama boys Wade Whatley of Tuskegee, Randy Walls of
Brundidge, and Ted Smith of Eclectic.

"Who would be the starting quarterback when Auburn opened
the season with Mississippi State on the road?" was the $64
question for Auburn fans. Many thought it would be Joe Bruner, a
six-foot five-inch, 205-pound highly recruited sophomore
quarterback.

Coach Lorendo, the offensive coordinator, surprised everyone
when he announced that Randy Walls, a six four, 205-pound
sophomore, would be the starting quarterback.

Lorendo made this comment on several occasions after the
season. "It was not what Randy Walls did for Auburn during the
1972 season, but it was what he didn't do. He didn't make
mistakes."

How would Coach Lorendo and the coaching staff put a
competitive team on the field in the tough Southeastern Conference

with practically none of their top offense players returning, plus having an inexperienced quarterback? Most Auburn fans were realistic saying, and knowing, this was probably not going to be a good year for the Auburn Tigers. "Hell, Sullivan, Beasley, Schmalz, and Yearout are gone and a lot of other good football players graduated with them last season." That is what most of us were saying and thinking. Auburn would be lucky to win a couple of games.

The Skywriters (the SEC sportswriters) who covered and toured the Southeastern Conference each preseason agreed with the Auburn fans, and most were predicting Auburn to win only two or three games. Auburn was picked to finish last in the Southeastern Conference.

Coach "Shug" Jordan made this comment before the 1972 season:

> *We will probably not be capable of scoring with the zip-zap suddenness of the Pat Sullivan-quarterbacked teams. We will rely more on a ground attack, which we worked on hard and patiently during spring practice. Our defense returns eight starters and our kicking game should be solid with kickers like David Beverly punting and Gardner Jett kicking extra points and field goals.*

> *The thing that impressed me most about our spring practice was the attitude and effort by the players. The players have created a challenge for themselves to have a good season. As much as they admire Pat Sullivan and Terry Beasley, they want to prove they can win football games. With all due respect to our opponents, and realizing it will take a superb effort on the part of all the players and coaches, we are not conceding anything.*

I had the opportunity to visit with one of the key players from the 1972 Auburn offense—"The Big O," James Owens. James was a big, strong, talented athlete who played five different positions in his career at Auburn. James told me, "The '72 team had a solid defense that could play with anybody. The offense had an inexperienced quarterback in Randy Walls, and we were limited in what we could do. But we had a good offensive line."

So Coach Lorendo decided the offense would only run four or five basic plays. James Owens, the powerful blocking fullback, would led the way for Terry Henley, the tough tailback and primary ball carrier. Owens was a key player at fullback as Lorendo molded this offense into a battle-tested unit. Leading the blocking was guard Jay Casey and All-SEC tackle Mac Lorendo (Coach Lorendo's son).

Other starters on the offensive line were center Steve Taylor, guard Bob Farrior, tackle Andy Steele, and tight ends Rob Spivey and Mike Gates. Their key plays were "20 Power" and "21 Power," which they ran over and over. Coach Lorendo challenged the offensive team every day at practice to become what they were capable of becoming, a winning team.

Auburn opened the season against Mississippi State in Jackson, Mississippi, on September 9, 1972. Randy Walls, the quarterback, related that whenever Coach Lorendo was talking to him, he was always looking up to Lorendo. Randy said, "I am six feet and four and one-half inches tall, and my high school basketball team listed me as six-five in the game program. But when Coach Lorendo was talking to me, I was always looking up at him. Coach Lorendo was a giant of a man."

The Tigers, using only three or four running plays, went out and successfully executed the basic offense they had practiced all spring. The defense was solid and the kicking game was excellent. Auburn controlled the game and won 14-3 over the Bulldogs. Terry Henley scored the first touchdown after a sixty-two-yard drive, and later James Owens scored on a fifteen-yard run after a seventy-yard drive. Henley finished the game with 136 yards rushing.

This game was a good start to what everyone knew was going to be a tough season for Auburn. It was obvious to all Auburn fans that there were not going to be any easy quick touchdowns this season. Everything achieved would be from using the old-fashioned game plan of one yard at a time.

Coach Jordan stressed over and over again to the '72 team, "Don't make mistakes or beat yourselves." And this team followed their coach's guidance, becoming one of the top teams in the nation with the fewest turnovers. When this team made it to the "red zone" (inside the opponent's 20-yard line), they scored almost every time during the season.

Auburn vs # 4 Tennessee

In the third game of the season, Auburn met the high-powered Tennessee Volunteers at Legion Field in Birmingham before 68,000 fans. Tennessee was ranked fourth in the nation, had won ten games in a row, and they were still smarting from the loss the year before to the Tigers in Knoxville.

This season, the Volunteers were loaded with one of the best offensive backfields in college football. They were led by the elusive Condredge Holloway, at quarterback, with two great running backs in Hanskel Stanback and Bill Rudder. (Stanback and Rudder would later be stars in the NFL, and Holloway would be an All-Star quarterback in the Canadian Football League.)

Fans were saying Auburn could not stay on the field with the explosive Vols. The Tennessee offense would just be too much for the Auburn defense to handle and the Tigers would have difficulty scoring against a strong Vol defense led by All-American linebacker Jamie Rotella.

The general consensus from everyone in the media was that Tennessee would win by two to three touchdowns or more. All of the SEC sportswriters picked the Vols to win big. One predicted a score of 35-7. The odds-makers were picking Tennessee by fourteen points, and a lot of money went down betting on the Vols to win this game by more than fourteen points.

In the first quarter, Auburn took over the ball on their own 19-yard line and proceeded to drive eighty-one yards to a touchdown. It took sixteen plays, with Terry Henley running the ball on twelve of those plays. Most of the plays were the 20 and 21 Power plays with guard Jay Casey and All-SEC tackle, Mac Lorendo, opening the hole and James Owens, the big tough fullback, leading the way by blocking the linebacker for tailback Terry Henley.

On a big fourth-down play, with a yard to go for the first down, guard Jay Casey, who was a vocal leader, announced in the huddle, "I can block my man." And Jay did for the first down.

Henley had run the ball six consecutive times on the 20 Power play. Bobby Freeman, Auburn's assistant coach and a former Green Bay Packer and Philadelphia Eagles star who was up in the press box, commented to Coach Lorendo down on the sideline by phone. "Hell Gene, let's run something else." Lorendo answered, "I am going to run this same damn play until they stop us."

Tennessee's All-American linebacker, Jamie Rotella, made a big tackle on a third down, slamming Terry Henley to the turf. With fourth and seven yards to go for the first down, Rotella was rumored to have said, "Now what are you going to do?"

Lorendo sent in the play from the sideline—20 Power, the same play again. With perfect execution, Lorendo and Casey opened up the hole and James Owens came blasting through, blocking the great linebacker, Rotella, as Terry Henley exploded forward for nine yards and the first down.

When Auburn made a first down on the Vols 2-yard line, Mac Lorendo told me that he, guard Jay Casey, and center Steve Taylor were down in position for the snap when one of the Tennessee defensive lineman commented, "I think I know what is coming." And right he was. Terry Henley took it in for the touchdown on the 20 Power play. This was the tenth play in a row Henley ran the ball.

In the third quarter, Gardner Jett kicked a thirty-yard field goal and Auburn increased their lead to 10-0. Tennessee finally scored late in the game on a thirty-yard pass for a final score of 10-6.

This was a team victory, with a lot of players playing a great game. The defense was steady and tough as they kept the pressure on quarterback, Condredge Holloway, all afternoon. There were a lot of heroes on the defensive side. In fact, all of them were heroes for holding one of the best offensive teams in the country to eighty yards on forty plays. Auburn's All-American defensive end, Danny

Sanspree, was a warrior for the defense, and he had a lot of help from teammates who contributed to the victory: Ken Bernich, Dave Beck, Johnny Simmons, David Langner, Bennie Sivley, Eddie Welch, Gaines Lanier, Bill Newton, Mike Neel, and Bill Luka.

Bill Battle, the Tennessee coach, was quoted in the Birmingham News the next day saying "Auburn whipped us physically up and down the field." Coach Jordan had this to say after the game: "It's mighty sweet to win when not a damn soul in the United States, including you gentlemen of the press, thought we could. Nobody, that is, except the Auburn football team." Shug added this comment, "I'm not going to single out any players. I'm simply saying that anybody who played for Auburn today played tremendously." Alf Van Hoose of the *Birmingham News* said, "This was one of the most beautiful afternoons in the long Auburn gridiron history."

A tip of the hat goes to the entire offensive coaching staff, which somehow molded this team with an inexperienced quarterback into battle-ready unit and upset one of the top teams in the country. The staff, led by Gene Lorendo, the offensive coordinator and assistant coaches Pap Morris, Doug Barfield, Bobby Freeman, Claude Saia, and Tim Christian.

Next up for the Tigers was Ole Miss, the eighteenth-best team in the country. Auburn had to travel back to Mississippi to play the Rebels and the Tigers were behind at halftime, but they came out strong in the second half with two big touchdown drives. The first drive was finished by a thirty-seven-yard pass from Randy Walls to Thomas Gossom.

After the defense stopped Ole Miss, the Tigers took the ball and, again, drove sixty-four yards in nine plays for the touchdown, with Randy Walls running the ball in from the five yard line. Auburn 19, Ole Miss 13.

The only loss in this unbelievable season came next in Baton Rouge before 70,000 fans in Tiger Stadium. According to Mac Lorendo, Auburn's All-SEC tackle and captain, nothing went right for Auburn from the moment they got off the bus. The undefeated and eighth-ranked LSU Tigers beat Auburn soundly 35-7.

But the Tigers bounced back with a 24-14 win over Georgia Tech at home. Next up was Florida State at home. FSU threw forty-two passes completing twenty-five, but had difficulty finding the end zone until the fourth quarter. Randy Walls, Auburn's quarterback, had a big day tossing two touchdown passes to Thomas Gossom for fifty-eight and twenty-nine yards: Auburn 27, FSU 14.

The Auburn Tigers continued their unexpectedly successful season with two big wins as they defeated the Florida Gators 26-20 and the Georgia Bulldogs 27-10.

And now it was time to face the No. 2-ranked team in the nation—Alabama.

CHAPTER TWENTY-SEVEN:

PUNT BAMA PUNT: DECEMBER 2, 1972; # 2 ALABAMA CRIMSON TIDE vs # 9 AUBURN TIGERS

Seventy thousand fans were crammed into Legion Field for this classic in-state rivalry game. Alabama was undefeated, and the No. 2-ranked team in the nation with a perfect 9-0 record.

Southern California, which was No. 1 in the AP poll, was facing a tough challenge from tenth-ranked Notre Dame. If Notre Dame could upset Southern Cal, the Tide could waltz into another national championship with an expected convincing win over the Auburn Tigers.

But first, powerful Alabama had to take care of business against the up-and-coming Auburn Tigers, a team with only one loss. Coach "Bear" Bryant and his mighty Crimson Tide team didn't think this task would be that difficult. Coach Bryant had made a comment on his weekly television show a week earlier that his team did not plan to lose to the "Cow College" (Auburn) they would be playing next Saturday.

The experts had predicted before the season that Alabama would repeat as national champs while Auburn, they said, would be lucky to win a couple of games. Remember, Alabama had defeated LSU earlier this season by the score of 35 to 21. This was the same LSU team that had beaten Auburn 35-7. The Bama fans believed. Many of them were wearing large metal buttons at the game that said "I Believe."

The odds makers had established Alabama as a sixteen-point favorite to win this game—meaning that, if you bet on Alabama, the Tide would have to score seventeen points or more for you to win your money. A lot of money was bet on college football games in this day.

What happened on this history-making Saturday? Auburn had a chance to score early in the first quarter when defensive back, David Langer, intercepted an Alabama pass. Auburn was first-and-ten on the Bama 4-yard line. A costly penalty and a bad snap on a field goal resulted in Alabama taking over on the Auburn 29-yard line. Some Auburn fans thought this was a sign of what was to come against their bitter rival, the Alabama Crimson Tide.

In the second quarter, Alabama running back Steve Bisceglia scored on a three-yard run. Roger Mitchell, Auburn's kick blocking specialist from Eufaula, Alabama, blocked the extra point for the Tigers. No one realized it at the time, but this was a huge turning point in the game. Bill Davis added a fourteen-yard field goal for the Tide in the first half to make the score 9-0. Wilbur Jackson, Alabama's great running back, added on a six-yard touchdown run in the third quarter to build the score to 16-0.

As the fourth quarter began, the Alabama fans were yelling and their players were holding up four fingers. The Tide team had been as good as advertised. They had been dominant for the first three quarters, and their fans knew the Tide had Auburn on the ropes. Now all they had to do was to finish the Tigers off and everyone would go home happy. "Roll Tide" could be heard throughout Legion Field.

The fourth quarter would belong to the Tide. Their fans thought back to a year earlier when the score was 14-7 with Alabama leading after three quarters and the Tide had rolled in the fourth quarter, winning 31-7.

Alf Van Hoose wrote in the *Birmingham News:* "Everybody thought it would be Bama laughter time, everybody that is except the Auburn's defenders, true architects of one of Dixie's all-time upsets."

With less than ten minutes on the clock in the fourth quarter, Auburn showed a little life as they drove from their 34-yard line across midfield down to the Bama 19-yard line. Then David

McMakin, an Alabama defensive back from Tucker, Georgia, made a big play for the Tide when he tackled the Auburn running back for a seven-yard loss.

Now it was decision time for Auburn. With the ball on the 24-yard line, it was fourth-and-eight for the first down. This was the Tigers' best offensive drive of the day. What should they do? Should they roll the dice and go for a first down that could lead to a touchdown? Or should they kick a field goal to finally get on the scoreboard?

Gene Lorendo, the offensive coordinator, and Coach Jordan, the head coach, conferred on the sideline. As they reached their decision to kick a field goal and put some points on the scoreboard, a strange phenomenon started to develop in Legion Field. The fans of both teams, Auburn and Alabama, started to boo loudly. Coach Lorendo told me, in his twenty-five years of college football, he had never experienced anything like this. The Auburn fans were booing because they wanted a touchdown. The Alabama fans were booing since a field goal and three points for Auburn would mean that Bama would have to score another touchdown in order for the Tide to beat the sixteen-point spread.

Gardner Jett kicked the forty-two yard field goal and the Tigers were on the scoreboard, 16-3. Auburn kicked off with 9:50 to play. Most fans would know the game was over if Alabama could make a couple of first downs and run the game clock down, leaving only a few minutes in the game. The Tide, behind their great offensive line and their wishbone offense, drove methodically down the field for three consecutive first downs. Then, on third down, Terry Davis, the Alabama quarterback, fumbled, but the Tide recovered the ball at midfield. Alabama was now facing fourth down and Coach Bryant made the decision to punt.

Auburn lined up with ten players at the line of scrimmage, as if they were coming after the punter, Greg Gantt, with an all-out effort to block the punt. Gantt, who was the All-SEC punter, had punted for seventy-two yards in his previous effort. He was a valuable weapon for the Tide.

Alabama was very much aware of Auburn's kick-blocking specialist, Roger Mitchell, especially after Roger had blocked the extra point on Bama's first touchdown. The Tide coaches had given Steve Bisceglia, a large running back, the assignment of blocking Roger Mitchell if he should penetrate the Tide offensive line. When the ball was hiked to Greg Gant, the white jerseys of Auburn all came forward with Mitchell and linebacker Bill Newton coming free. Bisceglia carried out his assignment by blocking Mitchell, but he could not block two Auburn players. Bill Newton flew straight to the ball and Gantt, blocking the punt.

David Langner, an Auburn defensive back who came from the right side with Newton, picked up the spinning football and raced to the end zone. Gardner Jett kicked the extra point and the score was 16-10 with 5:30 to play.

Auburn kicked off to the Tide. Alabama went back to their bread-and-butter offense running the wishbone behind All-American guard John Hannah and center Jim Krapf for three big first downs. Everyone was thinking at this point the game was over with the clock winding down—everyone except the Auburn defense.

On first down at the Alabama forty-two, Steve Bisceglia was stopped for a one-yard gain by Ken Bernich and Bill Newton. Terry Davis, the Tide quarterback, kept for five yards. With a third-and-four, the Tide was ready to roll to another first down and the victory. The Alabama Million Dollar Band was ready to blast out with a rendition of "Yea Alabama, Yea Alabama, You're Dixie's football pride, Crimson Tide, Roll Tide, Roll Tide."

Terry Davis, the Bama quarterback, rolled out to his right with the mighty wishbone offense in full control, powered by their great offensive line. One more first down and this game was history and in the record books. Davis had a trailing back, Joe LaBue, ready for the pitch out. As Davis read the Auburn defensive end, he was ready to execute the offense just like the play was drawn on the blackboard when Auburn's captain, Mike Neel, the rover linebacker (called the star position today), came out of nowhere to nail Davis in the backfield for the loss. The Tide would have to punt again.

A hush fell over Legion Field. Could the Tigers block their third kick of the day against the No. 2 team in the country? As Alabama lined up in their punt formation, the Auburn crowd came to life and the noise was deafening. The Tide players checked their blocking assignments. The ball was snapped. The Auburn white jerseys came forward. Roger Mitchell somehow got through the line, but Steve Bisceglia was waiting for him. Roger gave it everything he had as he soared high up into the air and over Bisceglia with his knees striking the big back in the helmet.

Gary Sanders, the Auburn radio play-by-play announcer, screamed that Roger Mitchell had blocked the punt. Yes, Auburn did block the punt, but it was not Roger Mitchell. It was linebacker Bill Newton again. Newton, a player who came to Auburn as a walk-on, had just made two of the greatest plays in Auburn football history. David Langner, bless his soul, scooped up the blocked punt and ran it in again for the tying touchdown. Gardner Jett came on to kick the winning extra point for the Auburn 17-16 victory.

And remember, Bill Newton's football career was turned around by Coach Gene Lorendo with this comment—"Is that all you've got?"

"Punt, Bama, Punt." Bill Newton blocks his second punt in Auburn's 17-16 upset victory over number two Alabama.

Alabama had one breath of life left, but David Langner intercepted, took a knee, and it was over for the Tide. Auburn had pulled off one of the greatest upsets in the history of college football.

In addition to blocking two punts, Newton, the 218-pound Auburn sophomore and linebacker from Fayette, Alabama, made twenty-two tackles, eleven of them unassisted. Ken Bernich, another Tiger linebacker, also had twenty-two tackles, ten unassisted. Added to that were great plays from end Danny Sanspree, tackle Benny Sivley, linebacker Mike Neel, and cornerback Dave Beck. The headlines for the *Birmingham News* read: "Lighting struck here twice at Legion Field in the fourth quarter."

Of the 72,385 in attendance, probably seventy-five percent were Alabama fans. A Birmingham policeman said he had never seen such a subdued crowd leaving an Alabama game. That could be because the Auburn fans were still in the stadium celebrating. Alabama was in shock…and Auburn was in "Gloryland."

Jimmy Bryan of the *Birmingham News* was in the Alabama dressing room after the game. Joe LaBue, the star Tide running back said, "I can't believe it."

What were the words to describe the mood in the Bama dressing room? Stunned disbelief! Mike Raines, Alabama's outstanding defensive tackle, said, "Losing a game like this will always be with you."

Coach Bear Bryant collected his thoughts, took a drag from his cigarette, and put the blame on his coaching. "I have been teaching punt protection a long time," he was quoted in the *Birmingham News*.

It is one thing to have one kick blocked, but it is another to have three kicks blocked in a game when you are the No. 2 team in the nation.

It is rumored that Coach Bryant fired his whole coaching staff after the game, and then hired them all back on Monday.

To add insult to injury, Southern Cal trampled No. 10 Notre Dame 45-23 to remain as the only undefeated team in college football in 1972.

Coach Paul Davis, Auburn's defensive coordinator, and his staff of Sam Mitchell, Joe Connally, Steve Greer, Jim Hilyer, and George Rose, had a great defensive plan. Coach Jordan, who had been a head coach for twenty-two seasons, rarely gave out a compliment in comparing one victory with another Auburn win. But in Clyde Bolton's Sunday morning article in the *Birmingham News*, when asked the direct question "Was this your greatest win?" he replied. "Oh yes." Shug then stated, "I don't know that I've seen a defense make a greater effort than Auburn did today. You've got to give our defense a lot of credit. They played well all day, but when we were practically out of it they blocked two punts and you know the rest."

Coach Jordan continued, "I've been on record this season as saying that this is the best coaching staff I've ever had, and I think they certainly deserve a lot of credit for the job they did today. In twenty-two years I have always hesitated to put one of my teams ahead of the others, but today I'm putting this team at the top of the list." Coach Jordan was named the SEC coach of the year for the 1972 season.

Coach Davis said of the two blocked kicks that won the game, "It was the same punt-block play we have used all year. We just had a little more desire to go and get it."

Coach Gene Lorendo came out of the victorious Auburn dressing room with a big cigar. He lit up and, with a smile, said, "Men, let's go back to our cow college and celebrate." (Later, after Alabama lost to Texas in the Cotton Bowl, Coach Bryant said he would rather lose to Texas ten times than lose once to the "Cow College.")

The Auburn players were certainly ready to celebrate when they arrived back in Auburn. In those days the big fad in high school was to roll a classmates home with toilet paper. Someone suggested rolling the big oak trees at Toomer's Corner in downtown Auburn. And the tradition began and continues today—rolling Toomer's Corner after a victory.

The rest of the story is that Auburn received a bid from the Gator Bowl to play thirteenth-ranked Colorado. Auburn lost their starting quarterback, Randy Walls, to an injury in practice before the bowl game, but Wade Whatley, who started the year as the fourth string quarterback and had never started a game, led the Tigers to victory by a score of 24-3.

Auburn players making the All-SEC team were running back Terry Henley, tackle and captain Mac Lorendo, defensive end Danny Sanspree, defensive back Dave Beck, and defensive tackle Benny Sivley.

Auburn finished this amazing year with a 10-1 record and ranked fifth in the nation. This team would be known to all Auburn fans for all time as the "Amazins."

Alabama lost to Texas in the Cotton Bowl 17-13 to finish with a 9-2 record and a national ranking of seventh in the nation. Alabama did end up winning the Southeastern Conference championship with a 7-1 conference record. Auburn and Alabama both only had one loss, but the Tide won the championship because they played one more conference game than Auburn. The difference in the conference championship was an Alabama victory over Vanderbilt.

The "Punt Bama Punt" upset victory of 1972 had to be one of the bitterest defeats in Alabama history. This game, along with three other victories, stand out in my Auburn memories of the Alabama series: The 1989 game, which Auburn won 30-20, was an historic moment for all Auburn fans as Pat Dye was able to force the No. 2-ranked Alabama team to come to Auburn for the first time. Auburn had always played Alabama in Birmingham, which was almost a home game for the Tide.

More recently, in 2010, Auburn and Cam Newton were down 24-0 at halftime to Alabama on their home field in Tuscaloosa, one of the most hostile territories in college football, when the War Eagles came roaring back in the second half to break Bama's heart by the score of 28-27. Phillip Lutzenkirchen caught the tying touchdown pass from Cam Newton.

And how can you top that historic win? In 2013, Auburn and Chris Davis found a way when Alabama missed a field goal with one second to play. Chris Davis returned the missed field goal 107 yards with excellent punt return execution by the Auburn team for the victory. Coach Nick Saban made this comment after the game, "I have never seen anything like that before."

We don't believe in miracles at Auburn. We depend on them. "We believe."

CHAPTER TWENTY-EIGHT:

A COACH AND HIS SON

MacLean (Mac) Lorendo was born on May 9, 1951, in Clinton, South Carolina. He was a short-timer there, though, moving to Auburn, Alabama, two weeks later with his family—mom Jane, father Gene, and two-year-old brother Cam—where they settled into a cottage in the Graves Center, a housing complex for scholarship athletes where Gene Lorendo was to serve as the new resident manager, along with his duties as assistant football coach.

Much of Mac's youth was spent with his dad around the football practice fields of Auburn, and he took to the sport like a duck to water. While a student at Auburn High School, Mac was a three-year letterman and captain of the 1968 Auburn High Tigers team. He was also named the Alabama High School Lineman of the Week after an outstanding game with Prattville his senior year.

Mac became a major college football prospect, having proven himself on the athletic field and also because of his excellent grades, which drew the attention of top universities including Georgia Tech, Duke, and the University of Georgia, all of which were recruiting him.

Both Georgia and Georgia Tech had former Auburn players on their coaching staffs who were familiar with Mac and the Lorendo family. Richard (Dick) Wood, a former Tiger quarterback, was at Georgia Tech, while Vince Dooley, the head coach at Georgia, and Jim Pyburn, one of his assistants, both of whom were former star Auburn players, were familiar with Mac Lorendo.

Coach Lorendo was busy with his coaching duties at Auburn on weekends, so Jane made the visits with Mac to Georgia Tech and

Georgia. Mac remembers overhearing his parents having a discussion (or argument) one night. Jane told Gene he should tell Mac who he should sign to play football for in college. Gene said he would not do it. "Mac should make his own decision."

Mac was caught in no man's land. If he signed with Auburn where his dad was the offensive coordinator, some would say the only reason Auburn signed him was that he was Coach Lorendo's son. But, if he signed with one of Auburn's major rivals and became a solid player, everyone would question why he didn't sign with Auburn and play for his dad. In the end, Mac made his own decision, committing to play for Auburn and his dad.

During his freshman year at Auburn University in 1969, Mac was set to play center on the freshmen team when a wrist injury in the first game kept him out of action for the remainder of the season. He started in 1970 as a defensive tackle and, later, was moved to offensive tackle. In the middle of the season, he was named a starter at offensive tackle. Mac made the AP All-SEC sophomore team in 1970.

In 1971, Mac was a key player on the offensive line, protecting Pat Sullivan, the Heisman Trophy winner. The Tigers won nine games and were selected to play in the prestigious Sugar Bowl.

Then came 1972, a season to remember for Mac and his teammates. He was selected as captain for a team that many knowledgeable fans predicted would not have a winning season. But the '72 Auburn team had an unbelievable year, upsetting two of the top five teams in the nation in route to a 10-1 season.

Mac Lorendo was a leader on this team, and was named first team All-SEC for his outstanding play as an offensive tackle. He was also named the national Lineman of the Week by *Sports Illustrated* on October 16, 1972, after he helped clear the way for 115 of the 150 yards tailback Terry Henley gained in the Tigers' upset victory over eighteenth-ranked Ole Miss.

Mac wanted to play for his dad, but he not only did that, he also exceeded his goal by becoming a star and captain of those 1972 "Amazins" and helping take the team to wins over highly favored Tennessee and Alabama, the 17-16 "Punt Bama Punt" victory being one of Auburn's greatest victories of all time. He was one of the few sons who played for their dads to achieve such high honors.

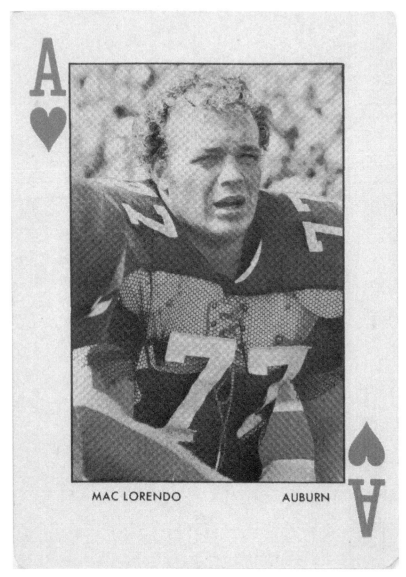

MAC LORENDO   AUBURN

Mac Lorendo, #77, All-SEC Tackle, Captain of the 1972 Amazins.

LORENDO

Auburn finished the season ranked fifth in the country when some folks did not think they would win a single SEC game. Mac Lorendo, the coach's son and a hometown boy, was a key player and leader for this "Amazin" Auburn team.

CHAPTER TWENTY-NINE:

LEWIS GRIZZARD: THE "AMAZINS"

From a Lewis Grizzard article in a December 1972 issue of the *Atlanta Journal*

I must admit the fact an Auburn man once saved my life has something to do with all this.

And I must admit further what follows will be completely biased. I simply couldn't allow the opportunity to pass without saying a few more words in behalf of the 1972 Auburn football team.

I got my first taste of sin at Auburn; or close to it, with a bottle of "Old Something" an of-age friend had purchased at the state store up the road in Opelika.

As I recall it now, I wound up in a lonely stall in the third-floor restroom of a fraternity house while the party roared onward downstairs.

There, as my life flashed in front of me and being grateful I had at least heeded my mother's words not to smoke, a kind Auburn student, a veteran of such incidents, wet-toweled me back to health.

I never got his name, but I have been forever grateful, and I have held a warm place in my heart for Auburn ever since, although I sought higher education elsewhere.

It is with that preface, I hereby state, I do indeed hope, Auburn wins its Gator Bowl game with Colorado, and that is the signal for all my poison pen pals from down the road in Tuscaloosa to start buying stamps.

When I think of Auburn: I think of purity for some reason. Of nothing to do but go to Toomer's and talk about what you talked about the day before and the day before that.

Of a low hippie ratio on campus, of real grass growing on the football field, of grown men in sweaters and open-collared shirts with 50-yard-line seats.

I think of Gerald Rutberg, a friend of mine, who edited the college newspaper at Auburn and used to ask me every day how I thought "The Big Blue" would do against whomever.

Of Bottle, Alabama, which is actually a suburb of Auburn.

Of the Yearouts (Gusty & Tommy), of Pat Sullivan, still the most exciting college football player I've ever seen.

Of Shug Jordan.

There are two remarks that still stand out in my mind concerning Shug Jordan, and those two-liners say it all. I once asked Harry Mehre if he thought Shug would quit coaching amidst the illness and the rumors. "Shug will coach as long as he can. He still loves the things most coaches don't think about anymore. He still loves the rah-rah part of this thing. He walks onto the field and hears all that War Eagle business they do down there, and Shug knows it's all worthwhile," said the old coach.

The first time I went to Auburn on business, I asked former Journal *colleague, Tom McCollister, what kind of interview was Shug Jordan? "Talking to Shug," Tom replied, 'is like talking to your daddy."*

When I think of Auburn, I think of the basketball coach, Bill Lynn, who looks and sounds like a hard shelled Baptist preacher, of journalism professor David Housel saying, "Auburn is in the best interest of the American dream." Of Buddy Davidson, who has never found either of the topcoats I have left in the press box. Or of Bill Beckwith, the worst golfer in history ever to score a hole-in-one. Of a golf tournament they had at Auburn once and the beer they carted to you on each tee, and of shooting 95 after being one-over through seven holes. That damn beer.

Of Randy Walls. Randy Walls was the quarterback in 1972, Sullivan's successor. He was the number-four quarterback at the end of spring practice.

"It wasn't what Randy did for us this year," said Auburn's offensive coach, "It's what he didn't do. He didn't make mistakes." (The Auburn offensive coach was Gene Lorendo.)

Actually, he did make one. So, excited was he about starting Auburn's first game at Miss. State, the young sophomore went out for the pre-game warm-up with his jersey on backwards. In the Georgia Tech game, Randy Walls didn't do anything right but win the football game. "I didn't know Randy Walls could run like that," somebody in the press box said after a thirty-yard jaunt that resembled your grandmother going after the mail. "He can't," was the reply, he can't. But he did.

When I think of Auburn.

I think of pasture land adjacent to the campus. Of my favorite Auburn line, "What do you get if you cross an Auburn Man and a gorilla?" A hairy county agent.

Of not being able to smoke in the Auburn Coliseum.

Of the old Sports Arena and Layton Johns.

Of Terry Henley. "Them FSU players bit me on the leg in the pile-up," said Terry Henley, college football's answer to Will Rogers. "They must not have had their pre-game meal." Did Terry Henley get tired carrying the football twenty-five times a game? "Hell, no," said Terry Henley. "I carried the football fifty times a day in spring practice."

When I think of Auburn.

I thought of unlisting my telephone number after an irate Auburn fan, a woman, called my home and said she hoped poison darts rained down on my body, and I died. Of a fellow from my hometown writing me and saying to never come back because "you stink, stink, stink." And all because I wrote Pat Sullivan was bush for not talking to writers after losing to Alabama. Of picking against Auburn all year in 1972, except once, the LSU game. Of

Owen Davis' line, *"Jordan waved his hand, and the Red Shirts of the Tide parted."*

Of Auburn students covering the whole town in toilet paper after the 17-16 victory over Alabama.

And somebody saying, "You mean they used both rolls?"

When I think of Auburn.

I think of the '72 team. It went 9-1 when it wasn't supposed to win three games; defeated three top-ten teams, stopped the nation's longest winning streak three times, got a bowl bid, and did my heart a lot of good.

Good luck in the Gator Bowl Tigers.

CHAPTER THIRTY:

LORENDO'S LAST YEARS AT AUBURN: THE 1973, '74, AND '75 SEASONS

As the 1973 season kicked off, Auburn was ranked thirteenth in the nation and Lorendo's goal was to rebuild the "Power-I" offense he had used so successfully in the 1972 season. He knew he had some big shoes to fill or replace with the loss of Jay Casey and Mac Lorendo in the offensive line, plus the power running of Terry Henley behind the strong blocking of James Owens.

This group of seniors had provided the leadership needed to make the difference in a lot of close games in the '72 season. Now Auburn had less power, but more speed and quickness with running backs Sedrick McIntyre and Mitzi Jackson and with Thom Gossom at wide receiver, but this team lacked the experience and power to win the close games.

After victories over Oregon State and Chattanooga, they lost at Tennessee in a thunderstorm before bouncing back to defeat Mississippi, lose to LSU, and win over Georgia Tech and Houston. Then came a big game with Florida at home. The Tigers fumbled seven times in losing to the Gators before a sell-out crowd by a score of 12-8. The only bright spot for the Tigers was the passing of Randy Walls to Thomas Gossom. This seemed to be the turning point in the season as Auburn went on to lose to Georgia, Alabama, and Missouri in the Sun Bowl.

Coach Lorendo's Power-I offense was struggling without a big blocking fullback like James Owens. The hottest offense in the country at this time was the University of Houston's veer offense, developed by Coach Bill Yeoman, an option offense using split backs. Auburn's freshman football team coach, Doug Barfield, was a strong advocate of the veer offense, which called for speed, quickness, and finesse. The Tigers had two of those quick, fast backs in McIntyre and Jackson. All they needed was an option quarterback, and they had one in freshman Phil Gargis.

Doug Barfield was named offensive coordinator in 1974 and Lorendo went back to the position of receivers' coach. Sure enough, Auburn rebounded in 1974 using the veer offense to win ten games, including a solid victory over Texas in the Gator Bowl. But, in 1975, Coach "Shug" Jordan's last season as head coach, Auburn won only four games, losing six, with one tie.

When Barfield was named offensive coordinator in 1974, it had to be a bitter pill for Coach Lorendo to swallow, especially stepping down after all of the glory he had led Auburn to in the previous seasons with Pat Sullivan, Terry Beasley, and then the '72 "Amazins." Coach Lorendo became yesterday's news. It was obvious to a lot of folks that Barfield and Lorendo were on a collision course and, in 1975, Barfield won out. Lorendo was named the recruiting coordinator. He would remain on the staff, but would come off the field as a coach.

When Shug Jordan announced his retirement after the 1975 season, three names were mentioned as candidates for the head coaching position. Doug Barfield was the favorite because of his age and the success of the '74 season. Coach Paul Davis, the assistant head coach and defensive coordinator who had previously been the head coach at Mississippi State and was an excellent defensive coach, was also mentioned. The third potential coach was Gene Lorendo. He had been Shug's right-hand man for twenty-five years and a key assistant coach for some of Auburn's greatest seasons. As one former player said, he was just a great football coach for twenty-five years at Auburn. But some said Lorendo was too tough, cussed too much, and chewed tobacco.

Ultimately, the position went to Barfield, who did not retain Lorendo on his new staff. Lorendo was disappointed and upset by the snub—after all, he had dedicated his life to coaching, and even though he was not on the Auburn staff, he was still a football coach—but he was smart enough to see the handwriting on the wall.

Coach Doug Barfield had a record of twenty-nine wins, twenty-five losses, and one tie in his five years as head coach. His defense was lacking, as evidenced by the following games: Auburn 27, Memphis State 28 in 1976; Auburn 38, Wake Forrest 42 in 1978; Auburn 22, Georgia 22 in 1978, a game in which Auburn rushed for 438 yards; and lastly, Auburn 0, Tennessee 42 in 1980. The one statistic that stood out was Barfield's record against Auburn's bitterest rival Alabama: Alabama won all five games by a combined score of 179 to 80.

Lorendo stated that Coach Barfield was not tough enough to win in the SEC, and the record bears out that the Auburn defense was not up to the task on the defensive side of the ball. Coach Barfield was replaced by Coach Pat Dye after the 1980 season.

CHAPTER THIRTY-ONE:

LORENDO JOINS THE COLLEGE OF EDUCATION STAFF

Though he was no longer a football coach, Gene's coaching career was far from over. In January of 1976, Lorendo made the transition to his new job as an instructor in the Department of Physical Education (now the School of Kinesiology) of Auburn's College of Education.

After being cut from the football staff by Barfield, it is safe to say that Lorendo was not in the best of moods when he arrived on his first day at his newly assigned office in the Auburn Coliseum at seven o'clock in the morning. When Tom Sparrow, Auburn's director of athletic facilities with whom Lorendo would share an office, arrived, Lorendo asked in a growling voice, "Who is in charge of making the coffee?" Tom replied, "No one is in charge of making coffee, but if you want coffee at seven in the morning, you will have to make it." Enough said. From then on, when Sparrow and the other athletic department staff arrived, coffee was always ready.

In the 1970s, the Auburn Beard-Eaves Memorial Coliseum on Saturday nights was probably one of the most popular performance venues in Alabama, or even the whole United States. Because the coliseum could seat as many as 14,000 fans for a concert, this was the spot for many of the big-time entertainers of the day to do a show in Alabama. Among those entertainers were Elvis Presley, the Rolling Stones, Willie Nelson, John Denver, Alan Jackson, Elton John, the Beach Boys, Jimmy Buffet (a former Auburn student), the Charlie Daniels Band, Alabama, Barbara Mandrell,

Wayne Newton, Bob Hope, Bruce Springsteen, and many others. Also appearing in the coliseum were President Gerald Ford, Muhammad Ali, Hank Aaron, "Pistol Pete" Maravich, astronaut and U.S. Senator John Glenn, and Soviet Union President Mikhail Gorbachev.

Needless to say, the Auburn staff was kept busy meeting the demands of these famous performers, and one day, as Tom Sparrow was preparing for a major concert, the agent for a featured singing group appeared in his office demanding fifty more passes for the group's upcoming concert on Saturday night. Tom reminded the agent that the group had already received fifty complimentary passes, as promised, but the agent insisted that the group needed another fifty. Tom explained in his cordial, southern manner that the concert was sold out, and no more passes or tickets were available.

As the agent kept insisting and Sparrow kept politely explaining there were no more passes, Lorendo was sitting over in the corner of the office buried in the morning paper doing the crossword puzzle and enjoying his mug of coffee. Finally Lorendo could not take it anymore. He lowered his paper and said to the agent, "The man said he doesn't have any more passes. Now get the hell out of here before I kick your ass out." The agent promptly left, but Tom confessed that he was a little nervous that Lorendo's comments would cause problems for this sold-out concert, which was to realize a nice profit for Auburn.

Susan Nunnelly (known as the "Nunn") was Lorendo's supervisor in the physical education department. Several of her colleagues expressed concern that she might have a problem supervising Coach Lorendo, but Susan said that was never the case. Lorendo did an outstanding job with his classes, was dependable and in complete control, and followed the syllabus to the letter. Most of all, the students loved being in Lorendo's classes.

Gene Dulaney was one of those students in 1977. He was taking softball as a physical education course taught by Lorendo. For part of the final exam, each student had to catch a fly ball in the outfield and throw the ball to an infielder at second base. Next, each student had to catch a ground ball at shortstop and throw across the diamond to the first baseman. Dulaney, who is left handed, had no problem catching the fly ball and throwing to the infielder at second base, but he had never played infield. When Lorendo hit a ground ball to him at shortstop, he easily caught the ball, but as he threw it to the first baseman, the ball soared over the first baseman's head and struck Lorendo's truck. Lorendo calmly said, "Fielding is an A. Throwing is an F." (Gene Dulaney is now a spotter for the Auburn Football Network broadcast team.)

In his new position, Lorendo was also asked to be an official for track and field meets held at Auburn University. Since he had participated in track during high school, junior college, and at the University of Georgia, this was an easy duty for him. Jerry Smith, former Auburn track star and assistant coach of the Auburn track team during Lorendo's days there, recalled that, when the Auburn team participated in dual meets at surrounding colleges like Georgia, Georgia Tech, Alabama, Mississippi State, Florida, or Ole Miss, Lorendo would always ask Coach Smith and Coach Mel Rosen, the head track coach, on Monday morning how they came out in the dual meet the past weekend. Coach Rosen would answer, "We came in last." Lorendo would usually comment, "That is not too good."

One day Coach Smith suggested to Coach Rosen, rather than saying we came in last in a dual meet, just say, "We finished second." When Lorendo asked how the team did in the dual meet the next Monday, Coach Rosen answered, "We came in second." Lorendo commented, "That is not too bad."

For one of the big track meets at Auburn with a number of visiting colleges competing, the university issued all of the track staff and those officiating a new golf-style shirt that read "Auburn Track Staff." For Lorendo, who was by then close to six feet three inches and 275 pounds, the XL shirt he received was way too small. The story is that Lorendo was not too pleased with the situation. He was so angry, in fact, that he threw a stopwatch he had been issued halfway to Tuskegee.

CHAPTER THIRTY-TWO:

A STEP DOWN TO PEE WEE FOOTBALL AND SCOTT PREP/LEE-SCOTT ACADEMY

Though Gene was able to coach and teach a number of sports in his new position at Auburn, he no doubt missed football. Perhaps that's why, in the fall of 1977, he took his college gridiron coaching skills to a smaller field.

That fall, Ron Anders had signed up to play football on a thirteen-year-old boys youth team in Auburn. It was to be the boys' first year of tackle football and their head coach was Allen Hunter, owner of a local Texaco station, who was assisted by Ronnie Anders, Ron's dad. After the first practice, which Ron Anders described as a typical "grandfather-type" coaching day, Coach Hunter announced to the team that the "Coach" would be there for practice the next day. All of the players looked at each other and wondered who is the "Coach?"

The next day Coach Lorendo showed up for their practice; a big man with a thick, white beard who, Ron recalled, spoke in a booming voice that sounded like God.

Coaches Hunter and Anders guided the defense with occasional suggestions from Lorendo, "Get more people up on the line of scrimmage," or the reverse, "Get more players back." Meanwhile, Lorendo coached the offense, instilling in them enthusiasm and encouraging them to play hard.

Though all the players were intimidated by Coach Lorendo, when Lorendo had a smile on his face, the players knew he was pleased with their play. And whenever one of the young players was struggling with a play or having a bad day, Lorendo would put his arm around the player and pull him aside for a few minutes. After a couple of minutes, the player was ready to get back in the action.

The team went on to win the league championship for the city of Auburn. At the end of the season, an all-star team was selected to play in the big bowl game, the "Shugar Bowl," which that year would pit a team from Auburn against a team from Columbus, Georgia, at the Auburn High School's Duck Samford Stadium.

For that game, Coach Lorendo decided to install the wishbone offense, and he chose Ron Anders to be the quarterback for the Auburn team. Auburn defeated Columbus 35-7.

Ron Anders said Coach Lorendo made an impact on his life and his teammates. He said Lorendo was genuinely interested in each boy on the team and, at the same time, taught the boys to be accountable to the coaches, their teammates, and themselves.

Can you picture how many coaches who had coached at the major college level for twenty-six years and had been a successful offensive coordinator could come out and coach a youth football team of thirteen-year-olds? This was Coach Lorendo. He was an exception. He was a "Coach."

In 1981, Coach Lorendo joined the coaching staff at Scott Prep as the offensive coach. Craig Ray was a running back and linebacker on this team. Craig had this to say about Coach Lorendo: "Coach Lorendo was from the old school of football. He believed in toughest and strong physical play."

Lorendo always had a chew of tobacco in his mouth. During scrimmages he would come into the middle of the field and spit before commenting on how the play was run. Because they usually ran each play from the same position on the field, after a while tobacco juice was everywhere. The center would try to sneak the ball forward a couple of yards to get away from the tobacco juice.

While some of the players were intimated by Lorendo, Ray said a number of the players, including the quarterback Tommy Bartlett and himself, loved Coach Lorendo.

LORENDO

Scott Prep of Opelika and Lee Academy of Auburn consolidated in the 1982 school year to form Lee-Scott Academy. Tom Meagher, a friend of mine in Auburn, played on the Lee-Scott football and basketball teams. Tom's grandfather, Jack Meagher, was the head coach of the Auburn University football team from 1934-42.

Coach Lorendo was the defensive coach on the football team. The offensive coach was John Niblett. Niblett's two sons, Josh and Tad, were always around the program. If the Niblett name sounds familiar, Josh Niblett is the head coach at Hoover High School, a perennial power in Alabama high school football.

Tom Meagher remembers Coach Lorendo complaining about the hot, humid days when they were practicing in August of '82. Lorendo may have looking forward to the cooler temperatures of northern Minnesota where he was planning to retire the next year.

Meagher recalled Coach Lorendo was always very vocal and demonstrative at practice. He remembers the coach being protective and always looking out for the players and was well liked by the players. Lorendo who also was the varsity boys basketball coach at Lee-Scott and, according to Meagher, they traveled to away games by car. Coach Lorendo drove his Chevrolet convertible and Meagher always rode with the coach. The basketball team had an excellent season before losing in the playoffs.

CHAPTER THIRTY-THREE:

RETURNING HOME TO MINNESOTA

Gene and Jane Lorendo sold their home at 864 Janet Drive in Auburn during the summer of 1983 to return to their home state of Minnesota.

Their friends in Auburn and throughout the Southeast thought they might be making a bad decision. But the Lorendos were moving back to the land of their roots, northern Minnesota, the "Land of 10,000 Lakes." Gene said "Everybody wants to go home," and home for the Lorendos was Minnesota, where Gene had grown up in Gilbert, a small mining village over in the Mesabi Range 120 miles east of Northome and Jane has been raised in Minneapolis. While most residents of Minnesota retire to warmer places like Florida or Arizona, the Lorendos did the opposite. They built a beautiful, contemporary home on Island Lake, located about five miles south of the small town of Northome (population 250) and just south of the Red Lake Indian Reservation.

Today, as you drive into Northome, you'll be greeted by a billboard reading "Heart of Big Bear Country" and a large wooden statue of a giant grizzly bear. Northome is mostly a summer vacation community in Koochiching County, located halfway between International Falls and Bemidji. This is also cold country during the long winters: Remember, Minnesota is the most northern state except for Alaska and over half the population of Canada live south of Minnesota.

Jane Lorendo's grandfather, D.R. Thompson, had built a large lodge on Island Lake in the early 1900s, a place where tourists from the Twin Cities came for summer vacations as well as for hunting and fishing and to enjoy its many scenic attractions. He named the lodge Danola Lodge for Jane's father and mother, Dan and Lola Campbell.

Gene and Jane Lorendo with dog at their beautiful home on Island Lake, Minnesota.

Jane Campbell Lorendo had spent part of her summers there ever since the 1930s, and it was there that she and Gene married in 1946. Through all the years of living in the South, the Lorendos had continued to return to Minnesota for their annual summer vacations so, when they decided to move back to Minnesota, they knew exactly what to expect and this was still their dream.

They quickly re-acclimated to life in northern Minnesota. Jane renewed her friendship with Jackie Bender Olson, a close friend since childhood. The Olsons had a farm in the area and, in earlier years, the Lorendo boys, Cam and Mac, had worked on the farm during their summer vacations doing haying and other farm jobs.

Auburn Artisan To Retire

THE NORTHOME RECORD
June 21, 1983

Jane Lorendo, associate professor in the Auburn University School of Home Economics since 1956, is taking her looms and things and going home. The Minnesota native, with husband, Gene. will return to Northome, where she expects to be just as busy on her own working with the various arts and crafts she's taught to so many. The Jane Campbell Lorendo Scholarship has been set up as a memorial to the uniquely creative professor.

Jane Lorendo with one of her many looms.

Jackie described Jane as an extremely talented person; a very gifted artist as well as an expert in weaving and pottery. While living in Auburn and teaching textile design at Auburn University, Jane at one time had seven or eight looms. She brought three of her favorite looms with her to Northome. One resident, city clerk Connie White, recalled that Jane "could weave or knit faster than you could imagine and carry on a conversation at the same time."

Gene became a regular at Kay's Cafe for his morning coffee and newspaper. This was the spot where everybody meets in town...the sheriff, mayor, farmers, loggers, and even a retired football coach like Gene. They discussed all of the problems of the world. Gene was known to everyone as "Coach."

Gene soon began writing a sports column for the local newspaper, the *Northome Record*, in which he wrote about the local and professional sporting teams in Minnesota. He was critical of the University of Minnesota Golden Gophers, calling them the "Golden Goofers." He was also hard on the Minnesota Twins and the Vikings. All of the local die-hard fans stayed upset with him. The year Bo Jackson won the Heisman Trophy, Gene wrote to his friend, Auburn's assistant athletic director Buddy Davidson, asking if he could get a photo autographed by Bo. When the signed photo arrived it said, "To all the gang at Kay's Cafe." All of the guys at Kay's Cafe were really impressed.

Gene had developed diabetes while at Auburn and, since retiring, had lost toes on both feet. This health issue now limited his mobility, but he was still determined to coach, spending one year coaching a local high school team in Northome and another season coaching a team in the neighboring community of Kelliher.

He also entered the field of politics and was elected to the local Ardenhurst Township Board. While he was in the hospital being treated for complications due to his diabetes, the board elected him chairman. This elected position kept him busy, as did travel, which he and Jane and Gene enjoyed during their years in Northome. They made a number of trips abroad, their favorite being a trip to Scotland.

One year their son, Cam, who has an interior design firm in New York City and is on the staff of the Pratt Institute, and his stepson,

LORENDO

Ross Campbell, traveled by car across country from New York to Northome. They stopped en route at Ewen, Michigan, where Cam's grandfather (and Gene's father) had grown up. (A number of the Lorendo's kin still live there today.) They visited some of the Lorendos who were still living in Ewen and also stopped by the local cemetery, where many of the Lorendos are buried.

Traveling on west, they made their way across Minnesota to Northome. Ross had never met his grandfather, so he was a little uptight about meeting the famous Gene Lorendo he had heard so much about.

These are Ross's words from the printed program at Gene's memorial service.

"One of the first memories I have of him is when he took Cam and me to the local coffee shop (Kay's Cafe) in Northome. This was a ritual for him, so it made it extra special for me. I was wearing one of his Auburn athletic shirts, which I still have to this day and wear on a regular basis.

I rode in the back of his pickup truck, called "Old Ugly," as we took the short ride to the bustling metropolis of Northome.

We parked outside of the cafe. I hopped out not knowing what to expect, and static with excitement. We entered the coffee shop and it was packed with people having their morning coffee. As Papa walked in the whole crowd turned around in their seats almost in unison said, "Morning Coach." This unexpected event made me even more giddy. I hadn't realized I was traveling with a celebrity.

We sat down in a booth and almost right away people started in with questions of who the two people were with him. He said with a proudness I have never seen, "This is my son and my grandson." At this point I realized I was someone special to him, and from that point on I would never refer to Papa as my "step-anything." He was my grandfather and no one could tell me otherwise.

So coming from not knowing what to expect from my Minnesota visit, I came away with a grandfather that I couldn't be more proud of. I've since been able to walk on the Auburn football field with him and meet the most famous of Auburn football players. The most wonderful experience I have ever had with this amazing man has to be the moment he afforded to me as kin."

In 1996, Gene and Jane celebrated their fiftieth golden wedding anniversary with a host of friends and all of their children—Cam, Mac, and Leah—present with their own families. One of my friends, Buddy Edwards, traveled from Atlanta to be a part of the celebration. This was a festive and joyous occasion for all of the Lorendos and their close friends.

Almost three months later, in early November, Jane Lorendo was traveling to Bemidji, the largest town in the area, for a doctor's appointment when she lost control of the vehicle she was driving, skidded off the road, and overturned. She was seriously injured in the accident and passed away on November 21, 1996.

After a long, tough "hellacious winter" in Minnesota without Jane, the love of his life for fifty years, Gene decided it was time to move on to another place. He considered moving back to Auburn, but with his severe diabetes and limited mobility, plus having congestive heart problems, Gene felt he would be better off living with family.

In the spring of 1997 Gene made the decision to move to Atlanta to live with his son and daughter-in-law, Mac and Liz, and their two children, Evan and Laina. Mac and Liz welcomed Gene into their home.

CHAPTER THIRTY-FOUR:

STORIES ABOUT THE STORYTELLER

Stories about Gene Lorendo abound. He had, after all, a personality as big as his size. Here are some of the ones I gathered while researching this book, stories that give insight into the man Lorendo was.

Thom Gossom Remembers

Thom Gossom, the first black football player to graduate from Auburn, captured Lorendo and his days at Auburn beautifully in his book, *Walk-On: My Reluctant Journey to Integration at Auburn University,* published by State Street Press and Best Gurl, Inc.

By Thom Gossom, Jr.

The following are excerpts from the book (pages 54-55):

Coach Gene Lorendo, the varsity offensive coordinator was fair; he treated all the walk-ons like dirt. He had been with Coach Jordan since the fifties. He had a deep, booming, scary voice. He could spit words that would make you piss in your pants. He stood six feet four inches with white hair and weighed 250 pounds, a Nordic Viking. A scary Nordic Viking. He was intimating and he liked being that way. He believed in breaking you down and remolding you in his likeness. If you were going to play offense, you had to learn to handle Coach Lorendo and his intimidating ways.

During one grinding practice, Coach Lorendo motioned in my direction and barked, "Hey you, you, you, and you, get over here." I scrambled over to Coach Lorendo panting, "Yes coach, yes coach, yes coach." My name was written on a piece of duct tape stuck across the front of my helmet; it read; "Gossom." "Yes, sir?" I asked. His pipe jutted from his mouth and he purposely mispronounced my name." Goossem," he growled, "You and your buddies get over there and warm up those quarterbacks." He pointed at the varsity offensive field where quarterbacks Pat Sullivan and Ralph Brock were limbering up for passing drills.

The drill was simple. Go out five yards and run a slant route by cutting back into the middle of the field. We'd all done it thousands of times before. But there was a catch. We quickly found out why the varsity receivers didn't warm up their own quarterbacks. Ralph could throw a rocket. He walked around campus with one of those hand squeezers that build up your forearms. He had huge Popeye forearms and biceps. When he threw it, the ball whistled. I learned that day that you had better get your head around quickly and get your hands up. If you didn't, you get drilled in the head. Bam! Guys would go down, get up woosy, stumbling around. That's why they used walk-on receivers. Walk-ons were dispensable.

My first time, I lined up. Ralph faked the hike from center. "Hut." I ran my route. Ralph let it go. Whoosh! The ball, a zinging missile, hit my hands. Crack! One of my fingers was dislocated. Pain shot through my body. My finger was bent in an ugly, painful grotesque shape. I held my bent hand with my good one. The pain had me hopping up and down wishing for some help. The trainer came over and calmly snapped the dislocated finger back into its original position. Crack! He slapped a couple of strips of tape on my fingers. Back in line I went.

(Pages 85-87)

Only once during the summer did we sit down as a family to discuss the potential scholarship. I explained that I'd done well, but that didn't mean I was guaranteed a scholarship. Also, I explained, if I did get a scholarship, it might not be until the *second or third year; it might not be this year. Daddy and Mama made it clear that school and getting a degree was their primary concern. If football worked out, fine. If not, I needed to make sure I concentrated on school. I assured them I would focus on my studies. One night I overheard Mama and Daddy. "I just hope he gets it," she said. Daddy countered, "He'll be okay. He's strong. Can't control what white folks gon' do. White folks gon' be white folks. He has got to learn to handle them."*

By the time, August rolled around. I had quit the job to prepare to go back to school. We still hadn't heard from the Auburn athletic department, but the grant and loan would pay my tuition, fees and rent; and I'd saved $500 to pay for my books. I was hoping that I'd get to eat in the athletic dorm from time to time.

The reporting date for football summer camp was August 13. On August 3, the phone rang and my mom answered. I watched as her round face lit up like the man in the moon. "Nice to meet you too," she said and beamed as she handed the phone to me.

"Hello," I answered. "Thomas. How are you doing, son?" It was Coach Lorendo!

"Oh. Okay, Coach, how are you?" I asked.

"Doing fine, Thomas," he replied. As usual he cut to the chase. "I am in Birmingham today doing some recruiting. You been working out?"

"Yeah, Coach," I answered. "Just got back this morning from running."

"You and your folks going to be home today?" he asked. "My dad is working," I answered. "But my mom will be here."

"What time does your dad get home?"

"He should be here by three," I answered.

"You think your mom and dad would mind if I stopped by?" he asked? "Well, no. I guess not," I answered. Then he dropped the bomb. "I've got something for the entire family!" The phone went dead. I hung up.

"What did he say?" my sister Kim asked. My mom, Donna, and Kim listened while I told them he said he,"had something for the entire family." Mom made the sign of the cross and Dad soon made it home. We told him about the call and he decided to go to his second job a little late. About 3:30 in the afternoon, a long, dark blue Ford LTD pulled into our driveway and Coach Lorendo, bigger and whiter than I remembered, rose from the car. When another white man emerged from the passenger side, I knew our neighbors would be coming over that day asking my mom why the two white men were at our house. Even before the men's shoes hit our driveway, our neighbors were all on their porches, trying to get a look at our visitors.

Nervously, I stepped out to greet the coach. He seemed bigger than ever. When Dad invited him inside, he filled up our living room. "Well," Coach Lorendo said, "We're very impressed with your boy here. We've been watching his progress and think he will make a fine player for our team." Dad got very quiet as he listened to the coach tell him the opportunities for a young man on the team. When the coach was done, he pulled out some papers from his case and offered me a full four-year scholarship to Auburn University.

I couldn't breathe. This was it! A chance to play ball at Auburn. I looked at my mom. Her eyes were brimming as she nodded at me. I knew that this was beyond her wildest hopes for me. She had made it clear that school was supposed to be my main goal, but I wanted to play ball for Auburn. I had written it down that New Year's Eve. What mom wanted for me was to get a great education and this man was offering us both our dreams on one piece of paper.

I took the paper and signed it.

Jim Foy and Indian Pines

Before Jim Foy, former dean of student affairs and one of the most beloved figures at Auburn University, died at the age of ninety-three in October of 2010, I had the opportunity to speak with him about Gene Lorendo.

Talking about Gene brought a big smile to Jim Foy's face and when I asked him if he had any favorite Lorendo stories, he said there were lots of stories or tales about Lorendo but his favorite was an experience he had while playing golf with Lorendo at the Indian Pines public golf course that straddles Auburn and Opelika.

According to Jim, he was part of a foursome playing one Friday afternoon with Lorendo and Coach Hal Herring along with another friend on the greens. They were teeing off from the white tees on what was then the first hole. (Today, this is the tenth hole). "Big Gene" Lorendo was up on the tee and, after a couple of practice swings, he was ready to tee off. He took a mighty swing and missed the ball. Jim Foy described how he did not dare smile, laugh, or even smirk when Lorendo turned around to face the other three players. As Foy tried to maintain a blank look on his own face, Lorendo broke in a big grin and then started laughing—so hard that Lorendo, Foy and the other two players almost fell on the ground.

Lorendo then turned to face the ball in his stance and pronounced, "I am going to hit this damned ball all the way to Opelika." With a powerful swing, he drove the ball all the way to front edge of the green. The scorecard for Indian Pines shows the distance to be 320 yards. A side note: The hole where Lorendo was teeing off is located in the Opelika city limits. Most of the course is in the city limits of Auburn. Yes, Lorendo did hit the ball all the way to Opelika.

A Visit With Pat Sullivan

David Housel, Auburn's retired athletic director, and I traveled from Auburn to Birmingham for an interview with Pat Sullivan. We were greeted by Pat's secretary, Dianne Blakney, and Jay Chapman, director of Football Operations at Samford University. Jay is the son of our Auburn friends Ed and Lee Chapman. I then had the opportunity to visit with Coach Pat Sullivan, the Heisman

Trophy winner and the head football coach at Samford University in Birmingham.

Pat told me about his junior year at John Carroll High School when they played Shades Valley High School. After the game when he came out of the dressing room, the big coach from Auburn, Coach Lorendo was waiting to speak with him. Coach Lorendo congratulated him on his play that night and told him Auburn was definitely interested in having him visit the campus and signing a scholarship with the Tigers.

From that time on, Coach Lorendo stayed close to Pat Sullivan in his career at John Carroll. A number of other colleges and their coaches became interested as Sullivan's career started to blossom. In Pat's senior year at John Carroll High School, he and his team had a big game with Fairfield and their outstanding player James Owens (who would later be a teammate and another Auburn star player). This game was played in a heavy rainstorm and several college coaches were on hand to see the game. Due to the horrible weather, all the other coaches in attendance left the game early. Coach Lorendo stayed through the whole game and was there to compliment Pat on his play after the game. Lorendo was quick to remind Pat that he was still there: "and if you don't sign with Auburn now—after I sat through this monsoon…"

Pat did sign with Auburn along with his friend Terry Beasley, the outstanding wide receiver from Montgomery. When I asked Pat how he liked playing for Coach Lorendo, he replied Coach Lorendo demanded that you give 100 percent. He said if you gave 100 percent, everything was fine. I inquired about play calling while playing for Coach Lorendo. Pat told me he called eighty percent of the plays during his time at Auburn. He said it is much different today.

Pat recalled how he rode on the second bus to away games with Coach Lorendo, who always sat in the first seat behind the driver. Pat said he enjoyed playing Jeopardy with Spence McCracken and Lorendo on the team bus.

One series Pat talked about was Florida. He and the Auburn freshman team had played the Florida Gators in Gainesville for their first game in 1968. Florida, led by quarterback John Reaves and wide receiver Carlos Alvarez, jumped on Auburn and dominated 54-17. Sullivan, Beasley, and teammates would remember this game for the remainder of their careers at Auburn.

The next season, the seventh ranked Florida Gators with their star duo would visit the Plains. Pat said he was sitting on a large tarp inside the dressing room when Coach Lorendo came over to speak with him just before going on to the field. Pat could tell Coach Lorendo was a little uptight about this big game. Pat said he told Coach Lorendo, "Coach, we are ready!"

Auburn defeated Florida 38-12. The Tigers intercepted quarterback John Reaves nine times in the game. Pat Sullivan and his teammates played an all-around great game as the Tigers won handily. Auburn with Pat Sullivan and Terry Beasley would dominate the Gators for three years in a row, winning in Gainesville by a landslide score of 63-14 (1970) and 40 to 7 the following year in Auburn (1971).

A Small World

On a Saturday morning in the fall of 2008, I was chatting with Mac Lorendo at our tailgate spot near Sewell Hall before an Auburn football game when a gentleman introduced himself as Marvin Ussery from Daphne, Alabama. Ussery, a 1974 Auburn grad, informed the two of us that he had a friend living in Auburn whose mother had gone to high school with Gene Lorendo in Gilbert, Minnesota.

Marvin's friend was Kevin Nolan whose mother, Agnes Nolan, graduated with Gene from Gilbert High School in 1939. The probability of two graduates of Gilbert High School living in the same small town in Alabama seventy years later is almost the same odds as winning the super lottery, especially in light of the fact that there were only sixty-two graduates in their senior class at Gilbert High School.

I contacted Kevin Nolan about the possibility of meeting his mother and soon after Kevin and Agnes, who at the time was a healthy eighty-seven-year-old, came to our home one Saturday morning for a visit. Her maiden name was Agnes Tahija and she grew up in the farming community called Hutter, which is near Biwabik, Minnesota. Biwabik is approximately six or seven miles from Gilbert, where Agnes rode the school bus for her high school education.

Later in her life, Agnes had lived with Kevin and his wife, Carol, for a number of years and, in 1996, they all moved to Auburn. One fall day in 1997 Agnes read in the local paper the 1972 Auburn University football team was being honored on their twenty-fifth anniversary at the game that week. She also noticed one of the captains of the 1972 team was Mac Lorendo. Since Lorendo was not a common name, she thought there might be some family connection with Gene Lorendo, with whom she had attended high school in northern Minnesota. She wondered if Mac might be related to the Gene Lorendo, who was an outstanding athlete at her Gilbert High School. She phoned the Auburn athletic department to inquire if Mac Lorendo was related to Gene Lorendo. Yes, Mac was Gene's son.

In April of 2001 she read in the local paper that Gene Lorendo had died on Easter morning in Atlanta. The obituary went on to say he was from Gilbert, Minnesota. Agnes told me Gene had beautiful red curly hair in those high school days, was a good student, and was a very popular classmate. She could recall the excitement at Gilbert High School and in the whole Gilbert community when their high school team won the district basketball tournament and went on to the state tournament down in St. Paul. Gene was the captain and one of the top players on the team. Gilbert lost to a much larger school from Minneapolis, but the whole town of Gilbert was very proud of their team.

(A side note: As of January 2015 Agnes is still living in Auburn and just celebrated her ninety-second birthday.)

Lee Cannon Remembers Jane Lorendo

When speaking to friends Tom and Emily Sparrow about the Lorendo family, they told me that if I wanted to talk with someone who was a close friend of Jane Lorendo I should get in touch with Lee Cannon. Like everyone who has lived in Auburn, I'd heard of

Lee Cannon, but I had never met her formally. Our good friends, Hank and Jane Elliott, (Jane is the daughter of Coach "Shot" Senn) had been close friends of Lee Cannon for years, so I decided to ask their help in contacting Lee. Hank and Jane most graciously agreed to set up a visit with Lee at their home. She was as sharp as a twenty-five-year-old at the young age of ninety-four.

Before she passed away on May 9, 2014, Lee Cannon was recognized as a leading socialite in the Auburn community. Lee had retired from Auburn University's School of Home Economics (now the College of Human Sciences), where she taught with Jane Lorendo for many years. Lee hosted a show on Alabama Public Television called "Today's Home" for fifty years and was the author of two classic cookbooks, *Southern Living's Quick & Easy Recipes* and *Menu Celebrations*.

One unusual side note Lee shared with me was that her brother, Richard "Doc" Ferrara, was a close friend of the television star Don Knotts back in their hometown of Morgantown, West Virginia. Don hung out at their home most of his free time and Doc and Don played in a band together while in high school.

When I asked Lee about Jane Lorendo, she told me, "Jane was an extremely talented, very astute person who taught art, pottery, and design textile during her teaching career at Auburn." Jane Lorendo was named one of the outstanding professors by the students in the School of Home Economics during her twenty-five-year teaching career at Auburn.

According to Lee, Jane probably had more looms than anyone in Auburn and was known for being able to carry on a conversation while weaving away at one of her eight looms. Most of the draperies, floor coverings, place mats, or hanging tapestries that could be found throughout the Lorendo home were designed and woven by Jane. Lee also told me that the Lorendos designed and built their home at 864 Janet Drive in Auburn.

According to Lee, Jane and Gene took dance lessons, which Gene really enjoyed because he loved to dance. Jane also loved the outdoors and enjoyed going back to Minnesota each year for their annual summer vacation in the small town of Northome and Island Lake where her grandfather had built a lodge. She especially loved to hike and canoe and, said Lee, Jane loved Auburn University and the small town of Auburn.

Though Lee said Jane was not enamored with Auburn football, but since Gene made his living as a football coach, she went to the home games and supported the team, players, coaches, and Auburn, usually bringing along her knitting materials to the football games.

After her death in 1996, friends, former students, and colleagues of Jane Lorendo established the Jane C. and Gene L. Lorendo Scholarship in Jane's memory to encourage enrichment opportunities for design students. The award is given to recognize and promote the qualities of creativity, insight, and imagination, all of which Jane exemplified, and to encourage special enrichment opportunities beyond the academic requirements for design students.

In doing the research for this book I discovered that Jane Lorendo's mother, Gladys Campbell, had moved to Auburn from Minnesota in the 1960s and was a housemother for a women's dorm, Helen Keller Hall, at Auburn University for five years. After retiring, she lived on Payne Street in Auburn until her death.

Also Jane Lorendo's grandmother, Leola Thompson, relocated to Auburn from Minnesota in her later years, living in a nursing home until her death in 1968.

Dr. Leah Rawls Atkins: A Glimpse into the Pre-Game Prep

I received word from a friend that Leah Rawls Atkins had heard I was in the process of writing a book about Gene Lorendo. Leah is a noted writer and author of several books on American and Alabama history. She is also one of Alabama's great athletes having won both the United States and World Championship in water skiing in 1953. Leah was the first woman inducted into the Alabama Sports Hall of Fame.

She is married to George Atkins, who was an all-SEC guard on the football team at Auburn in 1953-54, and later played for the Detroit Lions in the NFL. Leah and George were married in July of

1954. George joined the Auburn football coaching staff in 1956 as offensive line coach.

When the Auburn football team played out of town, coaches George Atkins and Gene Lorendo roomed together. They were close friends. One year they were playing Alabama in Birmingham at Legion Field on a Saturday afternoon game in which both teams were nationally ranked.

On Saturday morning Leah received a phone call from one of their four children who desperately needed a ticket for the game. She decided to see if she could get in touch with George and ask if he might have another ticket for the game. She was able to reach George at the hotel where the team was staying in downtown Birmingham. George replied he did not have any more tickets to the game.

About 15 minutes later Coach Lorendo called back and said, "I have one ticket for the game."

Leah said, "I will be over in thirty minutes to pick up the ticket."

In those days no one had a cell phone and most coaches did not communicate with their wives on game day. The wives knew the husbands (coaches) were totally focused on that day's game and were probably plotting strategy and doing Xs and Os while working on their game plan.

What did Leah Atkins find when she arrived at the hotel?

Coaches Gene Lorendo and George Atkins were watching Saturday morning cartoons.

(George Atkins passed away January 21, 2015.)

A Visit with James Owens

A friend of mine, Richard Guthrie, a former Auburn football player and dean of the College of Agriculture, asked if I ever had the opportunity to talk with James Owens about my Lorendo book. I said, "No, but I would love to visit with James." Richard phoned the next day and told me that James could see me Thursday afternoon.

LORENDO

James Owens, or "The Big O," has been one of my heroes of Auburn football. He was a member of the 1971 team, a teammate of Heisman Trophy winner, Pat Sullivan, and then a key player on the 1972 "Amazins" team. When no one thought that this team could win in the tough SEC, they proved all the experts and us die-hard fans wrong. They defeated two top-five ranked teams, plus two more of the top twenty-five teams in the nation. This team believed in themselves.

James said that he first met Coach Lorendo after his high school team, Fairfield, played John Carroll High in 1967. James' Fairfield team had beaten Pat Sullivan's John Carroll team. That Friday night, in the pouring rain, Coach Lorendo was there at the end of the game to congratulate both Pat Sullivan and James Owens on their play.

I asked James about his recruitment in high school. He related that a number of major colleges expressed interest in him, but in the end it came down to Tennessee and Auburn. Auburn assistant coach Jim Hilyer was recruiting James for Auburn, and James saw Coach Hilyer as a fine Christian man and they had a close relationship during his years at Auburn. James Owens' parents were strong Christians and believed in God. Another factor in his recruitment was that James' mother had never missed one of his high school games, and signing with Auburn meant that she would be able to continue watching him play football.

James was the first black football player to receive a scholarship at Auburn. He was a big, talented, and bruising All-SEC fullback on the surprisingly successful "Amazins" team. He and his pals, basketball player Henry Harris and teammate Thom Gossom, endured some difficult times during the integration of Auburn University, not only on the athletic fields but in every phase of college life. They stuck it out, though, and paved the way for the black athletes of today at Auburn University.

When I asked James about Coach Lorendo, he said, "Lorendo was tough and intimidating. He challenged us every day and instilled in us the desire to win. Coach Lorendo took boys and made them into men."

Today, James Owens is a retired minister. I wondered how he became a minister. He said that he felt God was calling him, but he told God, "I am not sure. I need a sign or signal for me to know that I should follow this calling." James confessed that he was an avid smoker at that time and really enjoyed his cigarettes, though his wife, Gloria, had encouraged him to stop smoking for some time. He recalled that the day before his talk with God, he bought a new pack of cigarettes. He smoked all of the cigarettes in the pack, except for three, and after talking to the Lord he put the pack of cigarettes down and never picked them up again. The Lord had helped him overcome his smoking habit, so he had received his signal from God, and he spent the next forty years spreading the gospel as a minister.

Today, Auburn has an annual award called the James Owens Courage Award. I can't think of anyone more deserving for showing courage in tough times than "The Big O," James Owens.

What a blessing it was to visit and chat with James Owens.

Lloyd Nix and the Lost Golf Ball

Lloyd Nix, quarterback and leader of the 1957 National Champion Auburn football team who was also an outstanding left-handed pitcher on the baseball team (his record as a pitcher in 1959 was six wins and no losses), told me about the time he was playing golf with Coach Lorendo and Coach Hal Herring.

They were playing at Indian Pines Golf Course (then the old Saugahatchee Country Club) and Lorendo tried to cut the corner on the twelfth hole, which is a par 5 with a sharp "dog-leg" left. Gene hit a line drive into the trees, the ball struck a tree, and bounced deep into the woods.

Everyone went into the woods to help Lorendo find his ball and Herring kept glancing down at his watch. Finally Lorendo said, "Hell Hal, we have all day to play eighteen holes. Why do you keep looking at your watch?"

Coach Herring replied, "Gene, I am looking at my compass...we may need it to get out of these woods."

Terry Henley-Every Ounce of Potential

I caught up with Terry Henley, who had become a top executive with Palomar Insurance, as he was leaving his office one weekday afternoon. Terry asked if he could phone me back in ten to fifteen minutes saying he was on his way to a late afternoon of turkey hunting.

When Terry called back a few minutes later, I mentioned I had missed him the previous Friday at the Tiger Trail induction program for former great athletes at Auburn. Terry had left the Tiger Trail program early to join his teammates in the Auburn Football Letterman's Club, who were holding a fundraiser for a former teammate, James Owens.

James Owens was the first black athlete to sign a football scholarship to Auburn. He was a key player along with Terry Henley on the 1972 "Amazins" team and their surprising 10-1 season. James was now a retired minister, and because of his declining health, he needed a handicapped bathroom.

Terry had to take a moment to say a few words about his former teammate, James Owens, who was a great blocking fullback on the 1972 team who had blocked many a linebacker and cleared the path for Henley as a running back. Henley stated James Owens was one of the most humble people he had met in life.

Terry said, "I love to be the center of attention." James Owens was just the opposite. He got the job done over and over and never expected any attention. You could tell that Terry deeply respected his teammate.

When I asked Terry about Coach Lorendo, Terry quickly pointed out that Coach Lorendo was never satisfied until he had gotten every ounce of potential out of a player. I told Terry that I had heard he and Coach Lorendo had bumped heads with some differences during spring practice of 1972.

Terry said yes, this did happen. Coach Lorendo prepared this team, with an inexperienced quarterback, for a ball control offense that would only pass the ball a few times per game. Basically,

LORENDO

Auburn only had three or four running plays with Henley running the ball and James Owens as the lead blocker. The favorite play was called the "20 Power Play" with All-SEC tackle Mac Lorendo (Gene's son) and guard Jay Casey blocking to open the hole and James Owens, the powerful fullback, leading the way through the hole and taking on the linebacker with Terry Henley right on James Owens' tail.

One day in practice Coach Lorendo was determined the offense would run the play exactly as he had instructed the team. After failing to execute the play to Lorendo's satisfaction, Lorendo had Henley and the offensive team run the same play twenty times in a row. Finally Terry scored a touchdown, tossed the ball to Coach Lorendo, and started running off the field. This was not a wise decision.

Lorendo said, "Where are you going?" Terry said, "Coach, we just scored," Lorendo countered with, "Get back out here and run the play until you get it right."

Henley said he and Coach Lorendo did reach a point where they both had mutual respect for each other. "Lorendo demanded you give 100 percent every day," said Henley. "If a player did not give 100 percent, Coach Lorendo would just brush the player off to the side. He believed you have to be tough to play the game."

The offensive team did get it right, and the results were seen in the 1972 season as the "Amazins" team finished with a 10-1 season and a Gator Bowl win over Colorado.

The defensive team for the "Amazins" should not be overlooked; they were solid all year. Led by Dave Beck, Danny Sanspree, and Benny Sivley, and a top-notch kicking game with punter David Beverley and field goal kicker Gardner Jett, the team finished the season ranked as the number five team in the country, when they had been picked to finish last in the SEC.

Several statistics about this team should be noted:

Auburn finished the season as the number one team in the country in fewest turnovers.

The Tigers scored every time they were in the red zone (inside the twenty yard line) except once during the season.

They didn't make mistakes and beat themselves.

This was a team that believed in themselves when everyone expected them to lose. They prevailed, even against mighty number two Alabama and "Bear" Bryant. They were the "Amazins."

A Visit with Jimmy "Red" Phillips

My dentist is Jim Phillips Jr., son of Jimmy "Red" Phillips the Auburn All-American end on the 1957 national championship team. I had told Jim Jr. I was interested in talking with his dad at a convenient time. Red Phillips was living up on Lake Martin north of Auburn.

A while later, Jim Jr. phoned me to let me know his dad, Red, would be in his office for a dental procedure the next day and he would be glad to visit with me afterwards.

Red Phillips was a great college football player at Auburn. He was an All-American end who played both ways, offense and defense, and was also a leader and co-captain of the team. Later he moved on to the NFL where he had a very successful career with the Los Angeles Rams making All-Pro.

I asked Red about Coach Lorendo, his offensive end coach. Red commented he was blessed with two outstanding coaches—Coach Lorendo on offense and Coach Joel Eaves on defense. Red told me all of the players were a little scared of Coach Lorendo. He said Coach Lorendo was "tough" and had this booming voice while Coach Eaves was quiet and reserved, but he really knew his business.

In addition to recalling the one time that his father came down to watch them practice, but never came back after seeing the tough love that Lorendo was doling out to his boy, Red also recalled what it was like living at Graves Center where Coach Lorendo was the resident manager. He told me there was never any doubt over who was in charge of Graves Center. Coach Lorendo was the man: No one messed with Coach Lorendo.

While at Auburn, "Red" enjoyed fishing after football season ended. One of his fishing companions was the president of Auburn

University, Dr. Ralph Draughon. Red said they would go out to a lake near Auburn, put in a flat bottom jon boat, and have a great time catching bream.

(Red's wife, Mickey, who was a beautiful Auburn majorette and a sorority sister of my wife, Joyce, in the Delta Zeta sorority, passed away in 2010. Red Phillips passed away in March of 2015.)

Erk Russell and Gene Lorendo-Great Athletes

Gene Lorendo and Erk Russell had been good friends since their time together on the Auburn football coaching staff from 1958 to 1962. Both men were great athletes. Erk Russell won ten letters at Auburn in 1946-1949, in four sports: football, basketball, baseball, and tennis. Lorendo lettered in three sports at Georgia: football, basketball, and track from 1946-1949. Lorendo coached at Auburn for twenty-five years (1951-1975) while Russell coached at Georgia from 1964 to 1981. Lorendo became the offensive coordinator at Auburn and Russell became the defensive coordinator at Georgia, so there were a number of years when Lorendo's offense was facing Russell's defense in the great Auburn-Georgia rivalry that began in 1892.

Lorendo and Russell's close relationship continued after Erk was hired by head coach Vince Dooley as the defensive coordinator of the Georgia Bulldogs in 1964. Gene and Erk would visit by phone several times during the football season. On occasions, Lorendo would phone Erk to congratulate Georgia on a big victory, and sometimes after a big loss to a team like Florida, he would say something like "We Georgia alumnae (Coaches Buck Bradberry, Joe Connally, and Lorendo) over here at Auburn are not happy with Georgia losing."

A couple weeks later it would be Erk calling to say the Auburn graduates (Vince Dooley, Jim Pyburn, and Erk) over on the Georgia staff were disappointed with an Auburn loss to Alabama. These ribbings and barbs were done in a fun manner and they continued between good friends.

Erk Russell left Georgia after not being named head coach for the Bulldogs in 1981 and went on to a fantastic career as head coach at

Georgia Southern where his teams won three NCAA Division II championships.

Lorendo and Erk enjoyed a lot of good cigars together and these guys—two of the toughest men you will ever meet—had another thing in common: They both loved to dance.

Nicknames with Kenny Howard

Kenny Howard, Auburn's legendary trainer and later an Olympic trainer who served the Tigers from 1948 until his retirement in 1980, shared with me that all head football coaches and most assistant coaches had nicknames. Many of the names the players called Lorendo during those long, tough sessions of winter workouts and spring practices could not be printed in this book. But a few can.

The most common nickname given Lorendo by fans and the press was "Big Gene." One former player called Lorendo, a "Damn Viking," a moniker that fit Gene Lorendo well. He was a giant of a man who was strong as an ox.

At the Minnesota State Teachers College in Duluth, Minnesota, Lorendo was called "Ranger," a term often used for folks who were born up on the Mesabi Mountain Range. During Gene's brief stay at Iowa State Teachers College he was called "Frenchy," a reference to Lorendo's French Canadian heritage. Some of his fellow students at Eveleth Junior College called Lorendo "Cager," in reference to his special basketball talents. At the University of Georgia Lorendo was called "Eskimo," a nickname given to Lorendo by Coach Wally Butts. A second nickname his Georgia teammates tagged him with was "Snow Bird," in reference to the snowy winters of northern Minnesota. Pat Sullivan recalled his first meeting with Lorendo when he described Coach Lorendo as the "Big Man" from Auburn.

Lorendo was not alone in collecting nicknames.

There was Coach Earl Brown, a graduate of Notre Dame who, as the head football coach at Auburn in 1948-50, won only three games. Brown was a flashy dresser who dazzled everyone with his bow ties and plaid sport coats. The players appropriately tagged him with the nickname of "Jim Dandy."

His predecessor, Coach Ralph Jordan, came to Auburn with his most famous nickname, "Shug," which had been given to Jordan by one of his high school classmates in Selma, Alabama. The story goes that Jordan not only lived in a community where sugar cane was a common crop in the 1920s, he was known for his fondness of sugar cane.

In the twenty-five years he served Auburn as head coach, the nickname given to Jordan by the players and coaches was "The Man," a well-deserved nickname for Coach Jordan in light of his prior service to our country in World War II. He had served as an officer in the Army in North Africa, Sicily, Italy, and the Normandy invasion, where he was wounded. After being sent to a hospital in England for treatment, he recovered and returned to the States only to receive orders for the Pacific theatre where he joined the allied forces for the invasion of Okinawa. Only a few hundred Americans served in both the European and the Pacific campaigns. Coach Jordan was one of those men. Coach Jordan truly was "The Man."

Coach Jordan was also a man of character who earned the respect of everyone with whom he came in contact. A few in his inner circle of coaches and associates, including Gene Lorendo, referred to him as "CJ" in private.

Another of Lorendo's close associates on the Auburn coaching staff was Coach Cary Lamar "Shot" Senn, the offensive line coach. One former player described Coach Senn as the toughest "little man" you will ever meet.

Speaking of Senn, his daughter, Jane, told me that her father Cary Lamar always said he was called "Shot" because he was such a good shot in basketball, but the real story is he got the name for some other reason from his Lambda Chi Alpha fraternity brothers. All freshmen pledges had to provide their father's name and the fraternity brothers came up with a nick name based on the father's name. Cary Lamar father's name was Charter which was Swiss. This evolved into "Shot."

Nicknames were a part of the times.

Dick Schmalz Remembers His Coach

I sent an email to Dick Schmalz telling him I was in the process of writing a book about Coach Lorendo and I would like to talk to him. Within an hour, I received an email back from Dick saying he would be happy to contribute to my effort to honor Coach Lorendo.

Dick stated, "I have many memories about Coach, some warm, some funny, some scary, but all good."

I knew Dick had attended John Carroll High School in Birmingham with Pat Sullivan. Dick told me he graduated in 1967 and Pat graduated in 1968, but Dick had suffered a knee injury his freshman year at Auburn and had to sit out the year. He implied that some of his teammates suspected that he might have been sitting out so that he would have three years to play with Pat Sullivan. Dick related he was about five feet ten inches and 160 pounds when he arrived at Auburn. By his senior season he was listed as six feet and 190 pounds. He was not heavily recruited, but he had a great career at Auburn.

With Terry Beasley, an All-American wide receiver, and Dick Schmalz, an All-SEC wide receiver, Auburn had two of the best pass receivers in the country. Beasley was the home run threat and Schmalz was the "Go to clutch receiver." When Auburn was facing a big third down and needed a first down, Sullivan would find Schmalz for the first down. Sullivan and Schmalz both knew what the other would do in certain situations on the field. They were on the same page.

Schmalz recalled one day at practice when the team was running sprints. Coach Lorendo, his position coach, yelled, "Hell Schmalz, you are so slow, you need to be over there running with the big linemen."

Dick told of another practice when the receivers were having a particularity bad day dropping passes. He was the only receiver who had not dropped a pass, then he dropped a pass over the middle. This must have been the tipping point for Coach Lorendo.

His pass receivers were having a bad day and even his most reliable receiver had just dropped a pass. Lorendo came running in and shouted, "Schmalz, you are chicken shit." Dick was a little taken back. But he stepped forward and said to the massive Lorendo, "Coach, I am *not* chicken shit."

After practice that day, Dick waited for Coach Lorendo to come out of the coaches' dressing room and said to Lorendo, "Coach, I apologize for my comment." Coach Lorendo put his arm around Dick and said, "I was a little too tough on you today." When Coach Lorendo put his arm around you, you knew everything was okay.

Dick recalled another special day in September of 2000 when he was asked to lead the Auburn football team in the traditional Tiger Walk before the Vanderbilt game. In those days, two former players or coaches were honored by being selected to lead the team down the Walk. Dick was excited and pleased when he was informed that Coach Lorendo would join him in leading the Tiger Walk. Because of Lorendo's severe diabetes and his loss of a number of toes, he rode in a golf cart with his son, Mac, as the driver. This was a very special and deserving honor for both Dick Schmalz and Coach Lorendo.

When Dick received a phone call from Mac Lorendo that his dad only had a few days to live, Dick phoned Coach Lorendo. He had a good conversation with the coach and they revisited some of their good Auburn times. As they finished their conversation Dick said, "Coach, I love you." Lorendo replied, "Dick, I love you."

Dick final comment about Coach Lorendo: "When I think of Coach Lorendo, I think of fear, love, and respect."

Murray Neighbors: Sneaking Into the Georgia Game

Murray Neighbors was a student at Auburn University in 1971 and he desperately wanted to see the big game between Georgia and Auburn. Unfortunately the game was sold out, so only 62,891 were going to be able to see the game with no television, plus those who were luckily enough to find a spot anywhere to get a glimpse of the game. All the student tickets were gone, sold out, and he could not afford the price of $50-$100 the scalpers were asking for regular $14 tickets.

Murray came up with a brilliant plan of how he might be able to sneak into the game. He had a fraternity brother who was a cheerleader. Murray decided to dress up like a cheerleader. He walked by the security personnel at the gate carrying two large megaphones, right into the stadium. The plan worked perfectly as he slipped right thru the security into the stadium.

Now he was in the stadium and on the sideline. He had overcome the first obstacle. He was inside the stadium. What would he do now that he was on the sideline with the cheerleaders? Could he fake it and make like he was a cheerleader, when they started doing their cheers? Would someone notice him and discover he was not a cheerleader?

Everything went along fine until the middle of the first quarter when Coach Lorendo noticed someone, who looked out of place on the sideline. Lorendo knew all the cheerleaders. Who was this person in an Auburn cheerleader outfit? Was he a Georgia spy? What was he doing on the Auburn sideline in this big game? Lorendo asked one of the team managers to find out, who is this guy. The manager came back and reported he is an Auburn student and a friend of the cheerleaders. Lorendo said. "Tell the SOB to get his ass off the sideline."

Murray quickly vacated the sideline and disappeared into the crowd with the 62,000-plus other fans, and what a great game it was for an Auburn fan. Murray did it.

Dave Edwards - A Tough Player

I had the opportunity to visit with Dave Edwards one day by phone about playing for Coach Lorendo. Dave had been a talented end who played both offense and defense for the Auburn Tigers in 1959, '60, and '61. He had gone on to a successful pro career with the Dallas Cowboys.

Dave told me he had played for two great coaches at Auburn: Coach Lorendo, who coached the offensive ends, and Coach Joel

Eaves, who coached the defensive ends. He emphasized that these two coaches were the greatest coaches he had during his playing experience, which included his time at Auburn and the NFL.

Those two coaches taught Dave the techniques he used successfully during his twelve years with the Dallas Cowboys. He said, whatever success he had was due to these two great coaches. He recalled that Lorendo instilled toughness in his players. Dave remembered one practice when it was pouring down rain, thundering, and lighting. Lorendo growled, "This ain't nothing compared to my days at Georgia with Coach Butts."

Dave Edwards only missed one game during his twelve seasons in the NFL. He was a tough football player. He went on to play in three Super Bowls for Coach Tom Landry and the Dallas Cowboys, including in 1971 when the Cowboys won the Super Bowl and NFL Championship, defeating the Miami Dolphins 24-3.

He was surprised to learn that Lorendo had played against Coach Tom Landry, the legendary head coach of the Dallas Cowboys in the 1948 Orange Bowl, where Texas defeated Georgia.

One of Dave's favorite memories at Auburn was seeing Lorendo with a big cigar driving his "A" Model Ford across campus with his large dog riding shotgun. Dave closed our visit with this comment of Coach Lorendo, "If anyone deserves to have a book written about them, it is Coach Lorendo."

Dave Woodward and the Air Conditioner

Dave Woodward was a big tackle who was living in Cedartown, Georgia, when he signed with Auburn just out of high school. (His family was in the mining business and they later relocated to Chattanooga, Tennessee.)

Dave received a surprise birthday gift from his mother in the summer of 1960—a window air conditioner unit. The gift was handy because none of the cabins in the Graves Center Complex where the football players lived were air conditioned, so Woodward's was the first in the complex.

One weekend Dave traveled back to Chattanooga to visit his family. When he returned to Auburn on a hot Sunday afternoon, he was surprised to hear his air conditioning unit running at full speed. Entering his room in the cabin, he found Coach Lorendo fast asleep in Dave's big vinyl recliner.

Dave came from a well-to-do family that had been successful in the mining business and his senior year at Auburn, they bought Dave a new Corvette. That year Dave also married Miss Auburn.

Lorendo's 1931 Ford Model A

In 1957, one of Gene's friends, a professor at the university, made him a deal he could not refuse. The professor had accepted a position at a college in the northeast and had made the decision to sell his 1931 Ford Model A sedan. Shortly thereafter Gene could be seen cruising around campus in his newly acquired Model A ride.

On one occasion I recall seeing Lorendo and Auburn engineering professor, Claude Layfield, ride up in his Model A to the Delta Chi Fraternity house. Layfield was the faculty adviser for the fraternity and Lorendo was a member of the faculty advisory board. Lorendo had been initiated into the fraternity and was now a member of Delta Chi.

I later learned that Lorendo's wife, Jane, and Layfield's wife, Mary, were good friends and both were professors in the Home Economics Department at Auburn University.

One of the most unusual sights in Graves Center or around the Auburn campus was to see someone other than Lorendo cruising around town in that Model A. For some unknown reason Lorendo allowed the "Yankees" to drive his vintage auto. Who were the "Yankees?"

Auburn had a football recruiting pipeline to New Jersey in those days and it was those Jersey boys—Ken Paduch, George Gross, Joe Leichtman, and Mike Simmons—who had special driving privileges. Apparently Lorendo trusted these players in the care of his prized auto. I was told these players would wash and polish the Model A and even change the oil for Lorendo.

Knowing Lorendo, it was one of the strangest sights at Auburn to see these players tooling around campus in his Model A. On the other hand, Lorendo was a "Yankee" himself...being from northern Minnesota.

Francis Sanda-A Lesson Learned

Francis Sanda was the manager of the Auburn Athletic Ticket office during some of Lorendo's years on the football coaching staff. After the football season was over a number of the assistant coaches, a few members of the athletic staff, and faculty would gather at the noon hour for a pick-up basketball game.

Bobby Freeman, Tim Christian, Sam Mitchell, Gene Lorendo, Buddy Davidson, Bill Oliver, Francis Sanda, and others would compete in a half-court game. The word was out: Do not drive the lane if you are playing on a team against Lorendo.

One day Francis saw the lane was wide open and he decided to go for it. As he drove the lane—wham! As Francis picked himself up off the floor, Lorendo said, "Don't try to drive the lane on me boy." A lesson learned.

Francis Sanda has been a familiar face at Auburn men's basketball games serving as the official scorer for almost forty years.

Softball in Auburn

When I starting talking to long-time residents of Auburn about Gene Lorendo, a number of these residents mentioned Lorendo's monstrous home runs in the Auburn men's slow-pitch softball league.

Joe Youngblood was one of Gene's teammates on the Southside Texaco team. Joe said Auburn was a small town and a close-knit community in those days in the fifties and sixties. Everybody knew everybody. They played together, went to church together, and

247

enjoyed living in Auburn. The softball field was located over behind the Frank Brown Recreation Center on Opelika Road. It was there that Joe, who is now retired from the postal service, but once delivered mail to the Lorendo's home when they lived at 864 Janet Drive, witnessed a number of Lorendo's home runs.

One of the other sluggers on the team with Lorendo was Jim Jeffries a large former Auburn football tackle. My friend, Hank Elliott, said he just happen to walk up one day as Lorendo stepped into one of his legendary home runs.

Another resident told of being present when Lorendo hit a colossal home run into the night in a late game. As a couple of fans scrambled to find the ball. The umpire shouted, "I don't have all night. Play ball."

Lorendo usually played first base, but if needed, he could play third base or pitch. He was described as a very competitive player who played softball the same way he wanted his football players to play: with an all-out effort.

Dennis Wilson, who was with the College of Education at the time, told of seeing a co-ed faculty softball game in which Lorendo was pitching for his team. The bases were loaded with two outs when the batter hit a screaming line drive straight back to Lorendo. The ball struck him in the shin and bounced all the way back to the catcher, Sandra Newkirk, who caught the ball and touched home plate for the third out.

Recruiting with Lorendo

On a Friday night in October of 1969, I met the Auburn University plane at Peachtree-Dekalb Airport in Atlanta. My assignment as alumni recruiter was to take Coach Gene Lorendo to see one of the top high school games being played that night in the state of Georgia.

This game was a battle of two highly ranked teams. Athens High School was the #1 ranked team in the state and Decatur High School of Atlanta was also a highly ranked team. Athens High was led by quarterback Andy Johnson, who was considered to be the top high school quarterback prospect in the state of Georgia.

Both high schools have a history of rich tradition and many great athletes, among them Fran Tarkenton who played at Athens High School, the University of Georgia, and was an All-Pro quarterback in the NFL. Decatur High School's list includes Frank Broyles, All-American at Georgia Tech who went on to have a distinguished career in coaching; Larry Morris, another All-American at Georgia Tech and MVP of the NFL championship game (his son, Shan Morris, was an outstanding defensive back at Auburn 1985-88); and many others including the Chadwick brothers, Walter, Dennis, and Alan.

Auburn at this time had an excellent relationship with the coaching staff at Decatur High School, which included three former Auburn players—Bill Van Dyke, '64; Don Lewis, '65; and Ben McDavid, '66. (Ben was the son of Joel McDavid, the former minister at Auburn United Methodist Church.) Auburn recruiters always received a warm welcome at Decatur High School.

This was an excellently played high school football game with Athens High coming out on top. Coach Lorendo was there to watch an end who Auburn was recruiting. He was also impressed with the play of Andy Johnson, the Athens High quarterback who was a leader, a tremendous football player, and an outstanding quarterback.

With a few minutes to go in the game, Coach Lorendo made his way down to the field and went straight to the end of the stadium where the Athens players would be exiting the field. As the players came through the gate, a large number of coaches from Florida, Georgia Tech, and Tennessee, along with two University of Georgia assistant coaches, were waiting for them. Coach Lorendo moved up close to the gate where the players were coming through one at a time and, when Andy Johnson came through the gate, Lorendo reached out and, much to Andy's surprise, grabbed him by the jersey.

Coach Lorendo said, "Andy, I am Coach Lorendo from Auburn. You played a great game tonight."

"Thank you, coach," Andy responded.

Lorendo cut to the chase quickly saying, "Andy, are you interested in visiting Auburn?" Andy quickly replied, "Yes sir."

"I will be in touch with you," Lorendo said.

The following Saturday, Auburn played Mississippi State at home. Pat Sullivan, Auburn's All-American quarterback, was standing next to Coach Lorendo on the sideline. On the other side of Lorendo was Andy Johnson. A lot of Georgia coaches and fans would have been concerned with what they were seeing on the Auburn sideline. Andy did sign with Georgia after the season.

Two years later, in 1971, Georgia and Auburn would meet in Athens for a big SEC battle of unbeaten teams. Who was the Georgia quarterback? Andy Johnson. Andy became one of the top running quarterbacks in the history of the University of Georgia with 1,799 yards in his Georgia career. He was also one of the top five rushing quarterbacks in SEC history. After graduating from Georgia he played in the NFL as a running back for eight years with the New England Patriots.

Thirty years later, Andy Johnson was playing in the annual Auburn-Georgia letterman's golf tournament. He and another Bulldog teammate were matched up against two former Auburn players. One of those players was Mac Lorendo, a former All-SEC tackle and Gene Lorendo's son. When Mac Lorendo said to Andy, "I think my dad tried to recruit you to come to Auburn," Andy laughed and commented, "Has the statute of limitations run out on my recruitment?" Not sure what Mac Lorendo replied, but, what he could have said was: "Andy, my dad played four years of football at Georgia after playing four years of football at three other colleges. Plus, he played one year of professional basketball in the National Basketball League, before playing three seasons of basketball at Georgia. Do you think the statute of limitations has run out on my dad's eligibility at Georgia?"

CHAPTER THIRTY-FIVE:

THE LAST DAYS AND GENE LORENDO'S DEATH

Lorendo was one of the most colorful personalities in the history of Auburn football. He spent twenty-five years on Ralph "Shug" Jordan's staff as an assistant, and he truly was Shug's right-hand man.

Lorendo had made a decision at the age of eighteen that his goal in life was to be a coach, and after playing football, basketball, and participating in track for eight years at four different colleges, he was able to achieve his ambition and coach for approximately thirty-five years. Gene became known to all he came in contact with during his career and after his retirement as "Big Gene" and the "Coach."

As Tom Sparrow, who had shared an office in the Auburn coliseum with Gene Lorendo after he came off the field and coaching staff at Auburn, was quoted at the beginning of this book saying, "Lorendo was the roughest and toughest SOB I ever met in life." But Tom went on to say that he had never met a man with a bigger heart than Gene Lorendo.

Spence McCracken, whose own father died while he was in school at Auburn, stated that the Auburn coaches were his adopted fathers—Coach Jordan, Coach George Atkins, and Coach Lorendo.

Lorendo's Last Auburn Game

On a beautiful fall afternoon in 2000, I was enjoying a tailgating experience at Auburn after a big SEC win over Georgia with friends Bob and Sandra Sarratt and Rob and Jan Slaughter.

Mac Lorendo walked up, greeted me, and informed me that his dad, Coach Gene Lorendo, was up in the lobby of Sewell Hall and would love to see me. I dropped what I was doing and headed straight to Sewell Hall.

Because Coach Lorendo had severe diabetes and had lost most of his toes, which limited his mobility and his ability to walk any distance at a time, the Auburn athletic department had provided a golf cart to transport Coach Lorendo to the stadium for the game and back to Sewell Hall.

When I arrived at Sewell, I found Coach Lorendo sitting in the lobby all by himself. Here, on a day when 85,000 fans were in town to watch Auburn play, was one of the legends of Auburn football sitting all by himself.

I sat down with Coach Lorendo and we had a great talk. Then I noticed two men entering Sewell Hall headed in the direction of the rest rooms. When they came back through the lobby one paused and said to the other, "Is that Coach Lorendo?" Both were former players who could not believe that this thinner, frailer man was their former coach.

As they embraced Coach with tears in their eyes and began reminiscing about their shared pasts, I excused myself and told Gene I would phone him the next week.

This had made my day. A great visit with Coach Lorendo.

The following week I phoned Coach Lorendo and we made plans to meet for lunch. I picked him up in my truck and we traveled up to Cumming, Georgia, to one of my favorite restaurants. After a lengthy lunch in which we talked about Lorendo's interesting life, I asked him, "How would you feel about me writing a biography of your life?"

LORENDO

Coach Lorendo sat with a far-away look in his eyes—almost like he was looking back on the seventy-eight years of his life—for what was probably only sixty seconds but seemed like ten minutes, before he responded. Then he said he would be pleased if I did a book on his life, on one condition. My mind was racing like a computer. What could that one condition possibly be? Coach Lorendo said: "The one condition is that none of my Auburn friends would be hurt by the book."

I have tried to adhere to Coach Lorendo's one condition.

At the End

With declining health due to congestive heart failure and a severe case of diabetes, Lorendo had reached a point in life where he knew his days were numbered. Clyde Bolton, a sportswriter with the *Birmingham News* and a friend to Gene Lorendo for more than forty years, wrote these comments in his column on April 11, 2001, just a few days before Gene Lorendo's death:

> *"Shug" Jordan's big, gruff assistant and I hit it off from the start. I'd drop by his office at Auburn and we'd chat about everything under the sun. When I phoned Tuesday, he greeted me with "My favorite sportswriter!" I'll admit I couldn't speak for a moment afterward.*

> *The strange thing Lorendo told me is that he doesn't feel terrible, yet he knows he is dying. "You can't fight it," he said of death. "There's no use worrying about it. It is just a phase. They say that after we die we go to a better place."*

> *He was always a great storyteller, and on his deathbed he still is: "Coach Jordan and Joe Louis were inducted into the Alabama Sports Hall of Fame together," Lorendo recalled. "Coach Jordan asked Joe 'Before a championship fight, what were you thinking about?' Joe said, 'Nothing. You can't do anything until the bell rings.' Words of wisdom from a sharecropper's son."*

> *So Lorendo waits for the bell to ring, the bell that will usher him into that better place.*

LORENDO

Furman Bisher, sports editor of the *Atlanta Journal*, wrote in his column in April of 2001 only days before Gene's death, "Coach Gene Lorendo, the Rough and Tough right-hand man of Shug Jordan at Auburn for twenty-five years, is in his last days."

Terry Henley, the star running back of the 1972 "Amazins," phoned to speak with Coach Lorendo when he heard Lorendo was in his last days. As they finished their conversation Coach Lorendo said, "Terry, I love you." Terry replied, "Coach, I love you."

Gene Lorendo passed away on Easter morning April 15, 2001.

From the *Decatur News* newspaper, Decatur, Alabama, Tuesday, April 17, 2001:

Lloyd Nix and Tim Baker, former Auburn players, can still recall the loud voice ringing over a football field, but they also remember the assistant coach who was like a father to them. Gene Lorendo, an assistant coach for Shug Jordan's twenty-five years as Auburn's head coach, died Sunday at age 79, leaving Nix and Baker to reminisce about "Big Gene."

"He was tough and he was fair, but if you worked hard, you had no problems with him," Nix said. "He wanted you to work hard and to give your all. If you didn't, he would send you on your way." Nix and Baker played on the 1957 national championship team and lived at Graves Center where Lorendo was the resident manager.

"He took care of us," Baker said. "He was like our daddy because he actually lived there with us. He looked after everybody."

Coach Buck Bradberry, an associate of Lorendo on the Auburn coaching staff, said the players who lived in Graves Center loved Coach Lorendo.

David Housel, retired athletic director at Auburn, had this comment: "Anybody who knows anything about Auburn football during Coach Jordan's era knows about Big Gene. He was as much a part of Auburn football as Toomer's Corner in his time."

CHAPTER THIRTY-SIX:

THE LORENDO LEGACY LIVES ON

The Alabama Legislature passed the following resolution on April 17, 2001:

MOURNING THE DEATH OF EUGENE LIONEL LORENDO OF ALPHARETTA, GEORGIA.

WHEREAS, herein recorded with deepest sorrow and regret is the death of Eugene Lionel Lorendo of Alpharetta, Georgia, on April 15, 2001, at the age of 79 years; and

WHEREAS, Eugene Lorendo, known by one and all as "Gene," was one of Auburn University's all-time most admired assistant coaches; he began his illustrious Auburn career in 1951 when he was hired as a member of the original staff of football's legendary Coach Ralph "Shug" Jordan; and

WHEREAS, Coach Lorendo enjoyed a 27-year career at Auburn, coaching many All-Conference and All-American players, many of whom went on to stardom in the NFL; during his tenure, the 1957 Auburn football team won the NCAA National Championship and, in 1971 as Offensive Coordinator, he coached Pat Sullivan, a Heisman Trophy winning quarterback; and

WHEREAS, his favorite team at the university was the 1972 team that is affectionately known in Auburn history as the "Amazins" that was co-captained by his son, Mac, an offensive tackle; and

LORENDO

WHEREAS, Gene Lorendo was born on December 7, 1921, in Gilbert, Minnesota, he earned an athletic scholarship to Eveleth, Minnesota, Junior College and later to the University of Georgia; and

WHEREAS, after attending a summer quarter at Georgia in 1942, he enlisted in the Coast Guard and proudly served our nation during World War II in the Pacific campaign; and

WHEREAS, he was discharged in time for the 1946 Georgia freshman team and while there he participated in and lettered in football, basketball, and track, and had the honor of playing in the 1946 Sugar Bowl, 1947 Gator Bowl, and the 1948 Orange Bowl; and

WHEREAS, after graduation, he joined the Presbyterian College staff as end coach and head basketball coach with his basketball team winning 19 of 29 games and the football team winning five of 10 games; and

WHEREAS, Gene Lorendo was preceded in death by his parents; his sister, Adele; and his beloved wife of 50 years, the former Jane Campbell; left to cherish his memory are his sister, Lorraine Looney; son, Cam and his wife, Lynn, and their sons, Graham and Ross; son, Mac and his wife, Liz, and their children, Evan and Laina; and his daughter, Dr. Leah Lorendo; now therefore,

BE IT RESOLVED BY THE LEGISLATURE OF ALABAMA, BOTH HOUSES THEREOF CONCURRING, that we are deeply saddened by the death of Gene Lorendo.

Sympathy is extended to his family and many friends, and it is directed that a copy of this resolution of sincere condolence shall be provided in tribute to his life and accomplishments.

Resolutions, Condolence

Lorendo, Eugene Lionel

A Fitting Tribute

The memorial service for Coach Gene Lorendo was held April 18, 2001, at the Church of the Hills Presbyterian Church in Duluth, Georgia. Many of Auburn's former athletes and coaches were present for the service, as well as a large contingent of former and present members of the Auburn Athletic Department.

Dr. Lawrence Wood, who conducted the service, made a strong point that Gene Lorendo was known to everyone at the church as the "Coach." This man who made the decision to be a coach in 1939 was still a "Coach" that day in 2001.

Laina Lorendo, Mac's daughter, spoke poetically about her grandfather. "For My Papa Coach, I love him when the sun comes up and when it sets at night. I love him with all my heart, when we are together or apart. I sit in his room and talk as we think of special times, sometimes we sit there and laugh, sometimes we sit and cry. To think of him in any pain makes me sit down and cry, then, to think of him with friends and family, in heaven in the sky. He always tells a joke about baseball in the sky, about how a friend came by to say, 'You're pitching next Tuesday.' It is the same for him, but football is the sky. He is coaching next Tuesday, and will again feel like a young guy. I love him with all my heart and will miss him every day, the way he comforts me inside, there is nothing more to say."

Evan Lorendo, Mac's son also spoke eloquently about his grandfather, emphasizing how close he was to Gene, how much he would miss him, and how much he loved and respected his grandfather.

Mac Lorendo closed the service with this comment: "Gene Lorendo was my father, my coach, my friend, my hero, and my Superman."

Where are the Lorendo Children Today?

Cam is a professor at the Pratt Institute in Brooklyn, New York where he teaches interior design. Cam and his wife Lynn have two sons, Graham and Ross.

Mac is retired in Atlanta after a career in telecommunications with the Bell Systems. He has two children, son Evan and daughter Laina.

Leah, the daughter, is a speech pathologist who teaches and coaches business executives to be dynamic and effective communicators. Leah resides in the St. Louis area.

A Phone Call from Cam Lorendo

One afternoon my wife Joyce and I were just finishing lunch when the phone rang. Joyce checked the caller identification on the phone and asked, "Do we know anyone in New York City?" I took the phone and said "Hello." The person calling answered, "This is Cam Lorendo. How are Joyce and you doing? I need a big favor from the two of you." I said we would be glad to help any way we could.

Cam then told us that his niece, Katy Coby, from Stratford, Connecticut, had applied to Auburn University. The response they were hearing from Auburn was that she might be ten to fifteen points under the SAT score required for acceptance. Cam said, "Don't you think they would give some consideration to the fact that her grandparents taught at Auburn for twenty-five-plus years?" Cam asked if we might look into the situation and see if we could be of help in getting his niece accepted to Auburn. We told Cam we would both see what we could do to help. Cam then added that Katy had dreamed of attending Auburn and she was going to be very disappointed if she was not accepted. Joyce and I told Cam we were not sure what we could do, but we were willing to try. Both of us contacted several friends at Auburn University. Afterwards, we agreed we were not sure if we had been helpful in this situation. Joyce said we should call Cam back and tell him it did not look good. I said, "Let's wait a week and pray for a miracle."

A week later, I phoned Cam. He answered, and reported the good news—Katy had received a letter of acceptance to Auburn that same day.

LORENDO

When the fall semester started in August, we received another phone call, this time from Katy's parents, Scott and Francine Coby, who were calling from the Auburn University Hotel and Dixon Conference Center inviting us to join them for a glass of wine and to meet Katy. We gladly went down to meet everyone. Katy was a beautiful young lady who was so excited to be at Auburn.

Four years later Scott and Francine called us again inviting us to join them at the hotel for another glass of wine and to celebrate with Katy her graduation from Auburn. This was a joyous occasion.

The Lorendo tie to Auburn continues. His legacy lives on.

Sources

Atlanta Journal and Constitution. Atlanta, Georgia

Auburn Football Media Guide, 1969-1972

Auburn Football Game Day Programs 1951-75

Auburn University Archives

Birmingham News, Birmingham, Alabama

Birmingham Post-Herald, Birmingham, Alabama

Bolton, Clyde, *War Eagle, The Story of Auburn Football,* Strode Publishers

Decatur News, Decatur, Alabama

Dempsey, Jack, *Armory Magazine,* Louisville, Kentucky 1946

Donnell, Rich, The Life and Times of Auburn's Ralph 'Shug' Jordan

Gilbert Herald, Gilbert, Minnesota

Gossom, Thom, Jr., *Walk-On, My Reluctant Journey to Integration at Auburn University,* State Street Press and Best Gurl, Inc.

Hollis, Dan, *Complete History of Auburn Football,* Auburn Sports Publications, Inc.

Housel, David. *Saturdays to Remember,* Village Press

Memorial Service Program, for Coach Gene Lorendo, Church of the Hills (Presbyterian Church), Duluth, Georgia

Montgomery Advertiser, Montgomery, Alabama

Newcomb, Richard, & Schmidt, Harry, *Iwo Jima: The Dramatic Account of the Epic Battle That Turned the Tide of World War II*, 2002

Pallette, Philip, *The Game Changer: How Hank Luisetti Revolutionized America's Great Indoor Game*, Author House, 2005

Quincy, Bob & Scheer, Julian, *Choo-Choo. The Charlie Justice Story*, Bentley Pub. Co., 1958

Sports Illustrated, 1964

Sports Information Director, Northern Iowa University

Sports Information Director, University of Minnesota Duluth

Sports information Director, Presbyterian College

Sports Information Director, University of Georgia

Thilenius, Ed & Koger, Jim, *No Ifs, No Ands, a Lot of Butts. 21 years of Georgia Football.*

Trippi, Charlie, University of Georgia, Letter

Van Dyke, Bill, *Georgia Trend* Magazine, April 2011

USS LST 789 (History), U.S. Coast Guard Association

About the Author

Kenneth Wayne Ringer is a native of Rome, Georgia and is a graduate of Rome High School. He entered Auburn University and the College of Engineering in 1955, and was the sports editor of the Auburn *Glomerata* (annual) in 1957 when Auburn won the national championship in football. There, he met Joyce Reynolds, whom he married after graduating in 1959 with a degree in Industrial Management. He received an ROTC commission in the US Army and served for three years in Germany.

Most of his business career was in sales. He joined 3M Company in 1968 as a sales representative and had a successful career with one of America's great companies. He retired from 3M in 2000 as an account executive after 33 years. After retiring, he returned to the business world to join his friend, Jim Thompson, and his company, Thomco, as sales manager for three years. In 2003, the Ringers moved to Auburn, Alabama where they are enjoying retired life.

The Ringers have three sons; Paul, John, and Patrick. They have three grandchildren; Alexandra, Gabrielle, and Ethan.

Great Nonfiction from White Rocket Books:

Lorendo
  (Kenneth Wayne Ringer)

Season of Our Dreams: The 2010 Auburn Tigers
  (Van Allen Plexico and John Ringer)

Decades of Dominance: Auburn Football in the Modern Era
  (Van Allen Plexico and John Ringer)

Assembled! Five Decades of Earth's Mightiest
  (Edited by Van Allen Plexico)

Assembled! 2: Earth's Mightiest Heroes and Villains
  (Edited by Van Allen Plexico)

Super-Comics Trivia
  (Edited by Van Allen Plexico)

**All are available in paperback
wherever books are sold
(as well as on Amazon Kindle)
or visit
www.whiterocketbooks.com**

Made in the USA
Columbia, SC
08 November 2018